ODD GIRL OUT

Laura James

ODD GIRL OUT

An Autistic Woman in a Neurotypical World

bluebird
books for life

First published 2017 by Bluebird
an imprint of Pan Macmillan
20 New Wharf Road, London N1 9RR
Associated companies throughout the world
www.panmacmillan.com

ISBN 978-1-5098-4306-0

Names and identifying details of some of the individuals and institutions
named in this book have been changed to protect their privacy.

'Is it Part of the Deal?', 'Somewhere in My Room' and
'Revolution Sam' courtesy of Tim James.
Grateful acknowledgement to Rune Lazuli for the use of
a line of poetry on p. 196.

9 8 7 6 5 4 3 2 1

A CIP catalogue record for this book is available from the British Library.

Printed and bound by CPI Group (UK) Ltd, Croydon, CR0 4YY

Visit **www.panmacmillan.com** to read more about all our books
and to buy them. You will also find features, author interviews and
news of any author events, and you can sign up for e-newsletters
so that you're always first to hear about our new releases.

For Tim

CHAPTER ONE

August 2015

'Can't you just enjoy the silence?' Tim sighs. It's a thin sound. Dark grey and unhappy.

'There's no such thing as silence,' I insist.

'Don't be ridiculous. You're over-thinking it. Again. Just stop talking, close your eyes and lie here in the dark.'

I know he's exasperated. There is tension in his voice.

He tries again, this time with a forced softness. 'You'll feel better if you just stop for a moment.'

Stop what? I don't want to make him cross, so I lie on the bed with my arms rigid by my side. Quietly, trying hard not to move. Trying to be silent. I need words. If I'm not reading words, listening to them or saying them out loud I feel jittery.

Not anxious, more a kind of scared. A sense of unease, as if something is going to happen. Like the rumble on a track that speaks of a train about to whizz by. My unease is not the fear of something bad, but something out of my control. Situations I can't control and events I can't predict confuse me, whether they are negative or positive.

There are good feelings and bad feelings. The good ones come in pretty colours and feel soft, like cashmere between my fingers. The bad ones come in shades of green and are jagged and spiky, like a piece of plastic that catches your finger and makes you bleed. Silence and nothing happening feel bad.

My sense is that most people chase the good feelings and either sit with the bad feelings until they pass or do anything they can think of to shut them down, to make them go away. I don't do this. I can't. I don't know how. The good feelings can be as overwhelming as the bad. They are just as big.

I can't name my feelings. I don't recognize them. Don't know what they look like. I know all the words that describe them, of course, and I like many of them. I like saying the word *optimistic*. I enjoy how it feels in my mouth. I like words that sound as they should feel. *Shocked* is a quick and brutal word and I imagine that's what the emotion must feel like. *Irritated* sounds scratchy and itchy.

No one uses the word *neutral* when it comes to emotions but that's how I want to live. I want to experience life in neutral. Not feeling anything much. For me, the absence of sensation is better than experiencing anything too jarring, too unexpected, too new. I want to move through life with no sudden movements. Sameness is my anchor. I want each day to unfold quietly and predictably.

Tim calls it *living in the grey*. 'If a painting can't move you or if a piece of music can't inspire you or take you to the depths of despair,' he has said, 'then what do you have? If you can't be moved to tears or lost in laughter, how do you know you're alive? If there's no joy and you strive only for an absence of fear or anxiety, then what kind of a life is that?'

It's my life, I think. Or at least it's my ideal life. It's not that I don't like music or paintings. I do, at the right time and in the right place. I don't like listening to music when I need to concentrate. The lyrics mix with the words I am thinking and it becomes a confused mess. Tim is right; I cannot be moved to tears by the arts. But surely that's OK? If I see a real person in trouble, I will do everything I can to help, so why does it matter that I can't weep over an imagined life?

In many respects – and certainly from the outside – my life is a good one. I have a solid marriage of twenty years and one where we never argue. I have children I love to spend time with and who love to spend time with me. I live in a beautiful house in a county that is easy to live in. I have an interesting job. I can do pretty much what I want to do.

I don't think feeling strong emotions would make *my* life any better. I can see why my being fiery or an adventurer would enhance Tim's life, however. He hates living in the grey. He wants the peaks and troughs. If anything, all I want to do is quash the fear that envelops me and takes over my mind at times. If I can just achieve neutral more often and learn to do the things that come easily to others then I think I may finally be content.

The world is an alien place to me. One full of dangers. I need to make sure they don't catch me out. I am aware of my fragility. Does everyone feel this? I'm not sure. If they do, how do they live with those feelings? I need something to distract me. I need words.

Tim shifts position on the hotel bed and takes my hand in his.

'See,' he says, 'isn't it great to just enjoy the nothingness of lying quietly in the dark? Doesn't it make you feel better?'

How can he actually believe it is dark? It isn't dark and it certainly isn't silent. A dull orange light from the corridor outside our room is seeping in under the door and the shards of brilliant blue-white from the day outside are piercing irritating gaps in the curtains. A red light nags at me from the smoke alarm above my head. There's a low-level electrical hum coming from the TV on standby on the wall at the end of the bed. Every once in a while footsteps echo in the hallway beyond the room. Voices bounce from the walls. Then, moments later, I hear key cards being pushed into slots and doors snapping open and slamming shut. Outside, there is a rustling in the trees and the distant sound of people playing tennis. I think I hear a dove. Do they have doves in France?

I go to reach for my phone to find out, and then remember I have promised to lie quietly and *enjoy the silence*. Tim strokes my hand. I hear his knuckles brush against the starchy cotton sheet.

'Isn't it great having no children to worry about? No demands on us. We can just lie here, get our bearings and relax until we feel like doing something.'

I feel trapped, as if I can't breathe. I need words. My iPad is on the floor next to the bed. There must be at least thirty audiobooks on it. I could be listening to a thriller, working out what will happen next. Or to a memoir, vicariously visiting someone else's life. I could be distracted from the million thoughts bouncing around my head. I swallow and hear the sound of them.

'We have two full weeks of nothing to do,' Tim says sleepily, turning over and away from me. After a few minutes his breathing becomes steady. I count to six as he breathes in and then seven as he breathes out. I count over and over until he begins to quietly snore.

I sit up and shield the screen of my phone as I check for any messages from the children. I feel an immediate sense of relief that I am now again on top of things. Tim doesn't stir.

He is silhouetted against the dark, his body curled up like a question mark. His head is freshly shaved and I have an urge to run my hand along it to see how smooth his skin feels. If I do, it will wake him up. He is thinner than he has been for a while. His weight reflects his all-or-nothing attitude to life and, although he is super-fit and sporty, it yo-yos and his mood goes up and down with it.

Currently it's at the lower end, which means he is comfortable in his skin. His happiness can be measured by the numbers on the scales at home. The lower the number, the higher his mood. I think this is, in part at least, due to the fact that a low mood, in turn, causes him to eat more and a cycle begins.

I get out of bed and pad quietly across the room. I gather up my things. My iPad, cigarettes and purse. I pick up my Birkenstocks and open the door as gently as I can. I feel a sense of relief. I am free. Free to be alone. Free to do whatever I want.

I should feel guilty. Weary from yesterday's journey from Norfolk to the south of France and a run first thing this morning, all my husband wants to do is spend an hour or so recharging before we decide how to spend our first day in Saint-Paul-de-Vence. He is making no demands. After a pretty stressful couple of months, all he wants to do is enjoy a moment of what he calls peace and quiet.

I turn his words over in my mind as I head for the pool. Peace and quiet. What do they actually mean? Surely even in the quietest place on earth you can hear yourself breathing? Peace is an even more elusive concept. The nearest I get to it is when I'm so caught up in researching something that my thoughts narrow down to a single point, like telegraph wires stretching to the horizon. Then, the ceaseless chatter in my head is dampened to a bearable level.

When I was a child I felt peace when I was spinning around in circles. I would beg my older cousins to cross their arms, hold my hands and spin me round and round. I kept my eyes open so I could watch the world whizzing past. After too short a time they would slow down and stop and wobble dizzily over to a garden bench. I would feel sad that it was over and would spin around in a circle all on my own.

The sun is fearsomely bright. I root around in my bag for my sunglasses. Shit! I left them in the room and I don't seem to have a key. I really can't risk waking Tim – it would be unfair – so I squint as I walk further into the sunshine.

The pool is a perfect rectangle, with sunloungers on each of its sides. They are neatly arranged. Just looking at them makes me feel calmer. As I open a small gate dividing the pool from the gardens I hear it squeak and then metal on metal as it closes. I can smell chlorine and suntan lotion and flowers. It's the scent of summer.

It is just after twelve-thirty and, with the sun at its highest, most guests have escaped the heat; only three couples have stayed the course. There's no one in the water, which is as still as a mirror.

I try hard to observe others, to notice how they behave. If I don't do this, most people – even those to whom I am closest – can become blurred outlines in my head. And when I am not with someone I struggle to form a mental picture of them –

even Tim or the children. If I don't focus on people they fall into the background of my world.

To my left, an English couple have moved their sunbeds to be closer together. She is reading *Fifty Shades of Grey*. He is lost in a thriller whose title I can't make out. The black cover, blood-red typography and monochrome photograph betray there's probably a detective involved. I picture him battling to solve his last case before retirement, while fighting the urge to down a bottle of whisky for breakfast.

On the opposite side is a girl in her twenties. She's with a boy a couple of years older. They are locked in their own bubble. Leaning in close, laughing, her legs are draped over his. I catch a little of their conversation. I think they are German. It may be their first holiday together; they are lost in each other, but not yet completely at ease.

An older couple in the far corner have the kind of French glamour you often read about. She is in her late sixties and is quintessentially chic, wearing a huge hat with a scarf wrapped around it. She and her partner are sitting in what I guess would be an easy silence. They seem relaxed, speaking only occasionally. How, I wonder, can that be comfortable? What do they do with all the thoughts that must be tumbling around their heads like washing in a machine?

I find a lounger at the far end of the pool – far enough from the French couple to avoid being drawn into conversation. I pull a huge umbrella this way and that until I achieve just the right amount of shade to allow me to see the screen of my iPad clearly. I take off my Breton top and immediately feel the sun on my back, hot against my skin between the straps of my bikini. I adjust the umbrella again and download my email.

The inbox fills with special offers from shops like John Lewis and Jigsaw, press releases for new books, furniture and beauty products, and lots of junk. I swipe to delete over and again until I am left with just one message. From my psychiatrist. The report I've been waiting for.

I light a cigarette as a waiter walks over. I ask if he speaks

English. He does and we begin the kind of exchange I have pretty much every time I order a coffee. Anywhere.

'How many shots of espresso do you put in a latte?' I ask.

'Two,' he replies, smiling, his eyebrows rising a little in the middle.

'And do you have whole milk?'

He doesn't understand the question and calls over a colleague, who arrives with an ashtray. They talk to each other in French and eventually agree they do have full-fat milk. I'm not sure if I believe them but I'm desperate for caffeine, so I ask if I can have a latte with the right milk and just one shot of coffee. They head off to a small bar on the far side of the pool in matching uniforms of blue shorts, white polo shirts and deep tan.

The hotel is perfect. It is exactly how it looked in the pictures I saw online. This is important. When a place looks different from how it has been represented on websites or in brochures I feel confused, as if I don't know which version to believe.

Tim and I agonized for weeks over which hotel to go for, but I'm glad we chose this one. I like its sleek, white minimalism, and its modernism is in contrast to the medieval architecture of nearby Saint-Paul. Worried about money, I was nervous about going away, but we found a good last-minute deal and the previous six months have been so full of stress and drama that we needed some time to reset.

I wait for my coffee to arrive, concerned that the order be followed to the letter. I thank the waiter and tentatively take a sip. It's OK. Not great, but OK. I can live with it. A meltdown has been averted and I feel my heart rate settle. I'm lying at the side of the pool with the Mediterranean sun warming my toes. I have an acceptable cup of coffee and I am about to lose myself in a ten-page report from the first psychiatrist to truly understand me.

Life seems OK, so I run through a mental checklist of things I should be worried about. This is our first holiday away from the boys, but at eighteen and nineteen they are perfectly old enough to cope and I've just had a sunny text telling me they're fine and the dogs have had a long walk. I worked hard before we left to clear away a lot of work stuff, so I have no deadlines to meet. I have been paid by a couple of my clients, so I don't need to panic about going overdrawn. I ordered oil for the boiler, had the septic tank emptied, had the gutters cleaned, the chimneys swept and the boiler serviced. And I have an OK coffee.

I scan the Word file on my iPad: 2,432 words on my autism. Confirmation of the diagnosis I was given last week. Confirmation that I am now officially one of the 700,000 people in the UK diagnosed with autism. Confirmation that I am one of the 1 per cent. For the first time in my life I am part of something. I am no longer alone. There are millions of others like me around the world. I have never belonged before. Now, perhaps, I can belong.

I'm still unsure of exactly what the diagnosis means and not knowing everything about it – absolutely *everything* – gnaws in my head. It is red, like danger. I think I'm pleased, but the words glowing from the screen in black and white – *Autistic Spectrum Disorder: Adult Asperger's* – pull at my stomach. I get up from the sunlounger and sit down at the edge of the pool, dangling my feet in the cool water.

I finally have some answers. Something to explain why I am the way I am. It is a relief, a vindication. I'm not mad, bad or sad – the terms some psychiatrists use to categorize patients. Rather, my brain is differently wired. My experience of the world is at odds with how most other people see it. As Morticia Addams once said: 'What is normal for the spider is chaos for the fly.'

I'm not alone. There are others like me, people who understand how a label in a jumper or a seam on a sock can cause a feeling so distracting everything else fades into the background. They would understand how it is to take everything literally. As a child, I had a real problem with sayings such as

'Has the cat got your tongue?' The first time I heard it, I was so alarmed I had to check my tongue was indeed still in my mouth. I regarded cats with great suspicion for a long time afterwards, which was a shame as, generally, I liked them much more than humans.

Others with autism would understand how I can sit down and write a complicated feature article for a magazine or newspaper, but cannot get it together enough to get dressed and make myself breakfast each day. They would know what it's like to be of above average intelligence, but never to have managed to pass an exam. To have been isolated and left behind at school. They would understand how if I have one thing in my diary I cannot do anything else. If I know I have a train to catch at noon, the hours between getting up and leaving for the station are rendered redundant.

These people (those now taking hold in my head, whom I want to meet, whom I need to know) would understand how getting a lovely surprise present is confusing and painful. They would know that all surprises – even those that I had been forewarned would be amazing – hurt, almost physically. A surprise is brutal. It comes without warning. It sparks the bad feelings.

A shadow falls over my outstretched legs. It's Tim. He is dressed in pale blue swimming shorts and a white T-shirt.

'Couldn't do it?' he asks, joining me at the poolside.

'Do what?' I wrinkle my nose as I often do when I ask a question.

'You couldn't relax enough to stay in bed.'

'No, sorry.' I put down my iPad and accept the cigarette Tim offers me.

'Just thought it would help,' he says, his head blocking out the sun. 'It's been crazy lately and you need to look after yourself by taking moments to relax whenever you can. We both do.'

I want to tell him that going to bed for no reason in the middle of the day is too weird for me to cope with. It's fine if

I'm ill or have, for some reason, been up all night. But having a nap feels wrong to me. Bedtime is around 10.30 p.m. and any other time makes me feel like I'm doing something strange.

Tim sits down next to me. 'What are you reading?'

I hand him the iPad. He scans the psychiatrist's report before giving it back to me.

'You didn't read it.'

I'm aware I sound harsh, so I playfully splash the water.

'It's too bright out here. Anyway, you told me at length what would be in the report. It's all we've talked about for what seems like weeks. Sorry, but . . . I said it would define you and I didn't want that . . . I just thought we were going to have some time off thinking about all of this.'

Outside of his work as a photographer – where he relishes creatively solving problems – Tim doesn't like dealing with difficult issues. I look at him easing himself into the water until only his head and shoulders are above the surface and realize he must be struggling to reconcile his view of me with the words written in the report.

I'm his wife of twenty years, the mother of his children, a colleague and friend, and now – all these years in and after a protracted period of ill health on my part – he finds out I'm autistic. It's a subject that – like most not directly touched by it – he knows little about.

He thinks *Rain Man. The Curious Incident. The Rosie Project.* He grew up in a time and place where problems were best swept under the carpet. If you don't talk about something it will cease to be. I do feel sorry for him. I know I am obsessive and it's probably torture for him to hear me go on about the same thing over and again.

He has already had enough and swims off to sit on some steps on the far side of the pool, half in the water, half out. He looks like a pink seal, reluctant to leave the water completely.

For much of my adult life I have been searching for answers to why I'm not like other people. Why I struggle with everyday life, why my body behaves differently, why my mind is never still. Having been endlessly misdiagnosed with everything from generalized anxiety to (and this is my personal favourite) 'bad luck', I guess I had just given up trying to find an answer.

That all changed when – completely by accident – I stumbled on the first of the three issues that affect my mind and body. The first of the unholy trinity of acronyms I now have after my name. EDS. POTS. ASD. (Ehlers-Danlos Syndrome, Postural Orthostatic Tachycardia and Autism Spectrum Disorder.)

Ehlers-Danlos syndrome is a group of rare, inherited conditions that affect connective tissue. I have type III, which means I'm hypermobile, my joints dislocate easily, my skin is super-soft and easily damaged, and I have serious digestive issues. Postural Orthostatic Tachycardia, which is often associated with EDS, is an abnormal response within the autonomic nervous system, the symptoms of which include a high and persistent increase in heart rate when standing.

I get up and go back to the lounger and Tim eventually swims over to join me. He dries himself off, lights another cigarette and settles back in the shade of the umbrella, listening to Arcade Fire on his phone. I admire his mindfulness. Like a Twelve Steps group member, he worries about only those things he has the power to change.

I'm just not built that way. I envy his quietness as I obsess about the structure of my brain, the pros and cons of genetic testing and why there is so little research linking autism and EDS. To me it stands to reason that if the glue holding your brain together isn't working properly, then you'll think and feel differently from others. The lack of data makes me feel dizzy and sort of agoraphobic, as if I'm in a vast sea and cannot catch sight of land.

I go to the room for my sunglasses. It's cool inside. I open my suitcase and fish out my notepad and pen, grab my sunglasses from the bedside table and head back to the pool.

Sitting back down on the sunbed with Tim to my right – eyes closed, toes tapping annoyingly to the music – I start to scribble in the notebook as I scour the web for research papers linking autism to EDS. When I reach the bottom of the first page of the notebook, I tear it out and put it on the empty sunbed next to me. I go through the exercise again, this time looking for information on the physical characteristics of autism. Again I tear out the sheet and place it above the first one.

I read that the definition of autism has changed in the latest *Diagnostic and Statistical Manual of Mental Disorders*, which was published in 2013. In the new version, the *DSM-5*, the terms *autistic disorder, Asperger's disorder, childhood disintegrative disorder* and *Pervasive Developmental Disorder – Not Otherwise Specified* (PDD-NOS) have been replaced by the collective term Autism Spectrum Disorder. This explains why my diagnosis of Asperger's syndrome is also a diagnosis of the all-embracing Autism Spectrum Disorder (ASD) or Autistic Disorder.

In the UK, it is the *ICD-10* (*International Classification of Diseases*), rather than the *DSM*, that is the most commonly used diagnostic manual. It presents a number of possible autism profiles, such as childhood autism, atypical autism and Asperger's syndrome. A revised edition (*ICD-11*) expected in 2018 is likely to align closely with the latest edition of the American *DSM*. It is likely therefore that Asperger's will be removed. As with the latest *DSM*, its diagnosis will be classified under autism.

I adjust the umbrella again to block out the sun and stare at the screen. I vaguely remember my psychiatrist explaining all this, but it got lost amongst everything else that happened that day. It's all so muddling. I like things to be clear and definite. This is murky and confusing.

I look over at Tim, desperate to tell him how hard I'm finding it all. I need clarity, but am wading through page after page of complicated medical language that is leaving me feeling out of my depth. I think he may be asleep, his favourite holiday hat covering his face.

I try to make sense of the information. I believe I have an understanding of how and where I struggle in real life, but I am finding it impossible to see how it all equates to what I read on the screen.

The diagnostic criteria refer to persistent deficits in social communication and social interaction in a number of contexts. They cite deficits in social–emotional reciprocity. I look away from the screen at the others around the pool, seemingly free from the need for such exhausting self-examination. I work out that *deficits in social–emotional reciprocity* refers to how conversations happen, how we share our stories, our emotions and interests. I know the way I do this is not typical. I tell the same stories over and again. I bore people by going on about my special interests. I don't initiate social interaction and often don't respond to invitations to do so.

I work through the list to see how this cold analysis of a disorder relates to me. It's not the first time I have tried to do this, but in the past I have failed. Confused and befuddled, I have given up every time.

My focus settles on *deficits in non-verbal communication*. 'That's true,' I find myself whispering. I find eye contact uncomfortable and have to remember to do it. My body language and facial expressions are often off. Often I feel I have to arrange my features into what I believe is the correct expression. I once asked my doctor about this and she said: 'There have been certain times when your expression was maybe not what I thought it would be, given what we were talking about. It's very subtle. A look or an expression or a twitch or something that was slightly different.'

The next section requires little dissection. I certainly do have *deficits in developing, maintaining, and understanding relationships*. This I have always known and recognized. I can often begin relationships, but don't have what it takes to keep them going. I rarely see any of my extended family. I can go for a year without seeing my parents, aunts and uncles or cousins. I find it overwhelming. I don't know how to be involved with the minutiae of other people's lives.

The *DSM* talks about *adjusting behaviour to suit social contexts*. 'I can't do that,' I mumble to myself. At a smart work meeting, I will curl myself up on a chair like a child. I will say exactly what I am thinking. If I feel worried about something, I won't be able to stop myself from saying it, even if it goes against social norms.

Tim asks if I'd like to cool off in the water. I hear the words, but I am too absorbed to consider replying. I pretend I haven't heard him. I think he knows it.

I have moved on to *restricted, repetitive patterns of behaviour, interests, or activities*. 'No I don't want to swim. I want to do this,' I whisper. Now this I can see. Yes, I have my patterns, but I feel comfortable with them. They reassure me and where is the harm in that? I need things to play out in exactly the same way in so many given circumstances. I line up my clothes and nail polishes in order of colour and feel uncomfortable if someone moves them. I repeat words or phrases in strange ways. Once, when I was in Germany, I heard someone in a restaurant say the word *stroganoff*. I found myself saying it over and again for the entire trip. In France one year, the word for the holiday was *hat*, which I recited for two weeks in a soft, plaintive voice.

The *DSM* talks about insistence on sameness and inflexible adherence to routines. My need to do so many things the same way is something people often remark on. It can drive Tim to distraction. My coffee shop routine; my need to use the same service stations on any journey. My need to have my bed just so. No green lighters. No keys on tables. Saying *Hello, Mr Magpie, how's your wife?* to every solitary magpie I see. There are so many. These things make me feel safe. Usually, I love them, but occasionally they imprison me.

The next line of the criteria talks about *highly restricted, fixated interests that are abnormal in intensity or focus*. These, I see now, are my intense or special interests. My passions. My *obsessions*.

It moves on to hyper-reactivity or hypo-reactivity to sensory input. I have sensory issues that can dominate my life. On bad days I feel under endless attack from the smells and sounds of my environment. I feel assaulted by bright lights. I can tell at the front door who has had a bath and what oil they have used. My children occasionally refer to it as a superpower. Conversely, I also seek out pleasant sensory experiences with an unusual fervour. I can't go through a clothes shop without stroking every cashmere jumper or soft, furry garment. Sometimes when I am working I have to go upstairs to find my favourite scent and inhale it deeply.

The definition of ASD refers to subjects being over- or under-sensitive to pain. My threshold is seriously high. I take no pain relief after any operation and didn't when giving birth to my children.

I need to process this information and wish I could talk to Tim, but he has had enough of feeling isolated while just a few feet away from me. The lounger is now unoccupied. How did I not notice he had left?

Instead, I pace in a short line from the lounger to the edge of the pool, wondering how all this information fits together and what it all means. I hear the English woman laugh and say something to her husband and I'm suddenly aware of how crazy I must look, pacing back and forth in a white bikini and Panama hat.

Tim eventually returns to try again. 'Shall we walk down to Saint-Paul and have an early supper there or would you like to get the bus to Nice?'

I was so lost in my thoughts I had almost not noticed he was near me. Now, seeing him trying to relax as his wife paces like a caged animal, I feel something I think may be guilt.

'Let's walk down and have a quiet supper,' I say, sitting down on the edge of his lounger, the wetness of his swimming shorts cold against my skin, causing me to itch. 'And I'll do my best not to talk about anything heavy.'

'It's fine. I just don't want it to be . . . well, the only thing we talk about.'

'But you don't like to talk about anything. You'd be quite happy saying nothing. If you can suggest something you would like to talk about instead of my diagnosis then I'd happily talk about that.'

The conversation ends there. Unresolved. It's as if we both know there will be no winner, only losers. We melt into the sunshine – Tim lying back with his eyes closed again, trying for a tan; me tidying away my notepad and then, searching for another distraction, reading a book about a young girl who has disappeared in mysterious circumstances. I like thrillers. I enjoy working out the answers and being proven right.

Later, feeling a little more relaxed and lazy from the sun, we begin the long walk down the hill into Saint-Paul. We discuss the houses we'd like to live in and Tim enjoys saying *bonsoir* to locals we pass en route.

Tim takes my hand and it suddenly strikes me that this is nice. We talk about what we see, about the weather, about what we're going to do while we're in France. It's pleasant and easy when for short periods of time I can manage to stop obsessing.

Saint-Paul is chocolate-box pretty. Nestling on a hill with medieval towers, cobbled squares, gift shops, clothes shops and bakeries, and locals playing boules in front of Pernod-branded bars, it is very quaint and very French. We find a restaurant with stunning views over the valleys of the Alpes-Maritimes down towards Nice and Antibes. It's not yet open but we are encouraged to take a table on the terrace. The woman who runs it is chatty and smiley and Tim talks to her in French. They are both animated, and listening to a conversation I cannot understand, the words washing over me, is relaxing because, as I don't speak French, I know I don't have to join in.

We order our food. I have many issues around food, but today the menu seems easy. I order a fish stew. There are no ingredients listed that I cannot cope with and, by the time it arrives, I'm ready to eat. It's easier to eat on holiday when there's not much else to think about and interruptions of any kind don't send my hunger scurrying. At home I find it almost impossible to feed myself consistently and I end up surviving on coffee, cigarettes and chocolate.

A cat weaves its way around the tables. It is lean and insistent, subtly striped, with oversized ears. It has an Egyptian appearance. I feed it small pieces of fish and it rubs its face against my fingers, purring loudly.

'Do you want to talk about it?' Tim asks, when the cat finally jumps from my lap to try its luck with a couple who have just sat down. They are Americans and they complain to the restaurant owner about the hygiene issues of an animal around food.

'About what?'

'Your diagnosis,' he says. He still cannot comfortably bring himself to say the *A* word.

'If you want to,' I reply. I know it's hard for him, so I'm grateful he's made the first move. I push my plate to one side and reach for a cigarette. I see Tim scowl at another half-eaten meal in front of me. 'I just feel as if all my life I have thought I am a dog and have now been given the bombshell news that I am actually a cat.'

Tim laughs, but kindly. He pours me some water and tops up his own glass.

'I don't know which bits of my personality are down to the autism and which bits are inherently me.'

'Why does it matter?'

'I don't know,' I reply. 'But for some reason it really does.'

The waitress comes over and Tim orders another bottle of water and a beer. I wait for her to leave.

'All my life I've tried to hide my weirdness from others. I've tried to pretend to be just like everyone else and now I don't know what to do or how to behave. I feel lost.'

I take a sip of water and enjoy the feeling of the gentle warmth of the setting sun on my back.

I reel off facts. 'Did you know 87 per cent of people with an autism diagnosis are unemployed? Or that 42 per cent of autistic women have previously been misdiagnosed. Can you believe that the vast majority of research has only looked at boys? Also, I found out the life expectancy of an autistic person is between ten and thirty years shorter than for a neurotypical person. I will probably die way before you.'

This is a classic autistic *info dump*. I have all these thoughts in my head and I have to get them out. Even if the listener is so bored they are contemplating throwing themselves off a cliff to get away from my incessant chatter, I simply cannot stop.

Something crosses Tim's face. I try to think what it means. I spend my life trying to work out what Tim is feeling or what his mood is. He seems something, but I'm not sure what. Bored perhaps. Yes, I'm sure he's bored. He is bored. He doesn't respond well to random facts or statistics and he is fidgety. He's looking at me, but also around the restaurant, sometimes directly at me but at other times at the view over the valley towards the Mediterranean or at other guests slowly filling up the terrace. I can't stop talking.

'Part of me just can't believe this is happening. To me, I mean, I would never in a million years have thought I might be autistic. It just seems so surreal and I can't think about any-thing else . . .'

Tim cuts in. 'What are you going to do? Now you know.'

His beer arrives and I wait for the waitress to leave. 'I think I'm going to try to concentrate on having a lovely holiday and not driving you too mad.'

The words sound rehearsed. It's what Tim wants to hear. He raises his bottle of Peroni as if toasting the idea of two weeks without difficult conversations. We each find somewhere else to look before Tim breaks the silence.

'Oh, come on. You don't mean that. It's not going to happen. And what about later? I'm worried that you'll become your diagnosis. Defined by it. That things will change and you will never be the same as you were before.'

It's rare for Tim to confess to a worry, so I feel I have to take it seriously. I think about it for a while. I know I'm going to start seeing a psychologist. The first appointment is already booked. I have a real sense of hope that this time therapy will fix me. Now we know what we're dealing with, now the problem is out in the open. Surely there is a way to make it not matter anymore. I know there's no quick fix – no pill I can take – but if I work hard enough the therapy will change my life. Of that I'm sure.

'I'm going to get better,' I say. 'I will become the best possible me.'

We stare at each other for a moment. He is going to say something deep, something profound. He is going to tell me that everything is going to be OK. That he loves me. Instead he starts to laugh, quietly at first, then louder until he is laughing uncontrollably, with tears in his eyes. I, too, find myself giggling, losing control. Other diners in the restaurant are staring at us, but we cannot stop laughing.

Suddenly everything feels lighter. We're still the same people. I'm the same as I was before my diagnosis and we're not the sort of couple that allows each other to get away with spouting pompous nonsense about finding our best possible selves.

'It will be all right, Boo,' he says. 'You just need to stop obsessing and realize that – diagnosis or no diagnosis – this is who you are.'

I think about this in the long taxi ride up the hill back to the hotel. Tim's arm is across my shoulder. He looks what I think is content in the arc of headlights streaming into the car.

I'm confused. *This doesn't have to be who I am.* I can be different. Better. Less scared. I can be fixed.

Tim is saying that I am who I am and nothing is going to change me. But at the same time he is trying to make me be a different person. He is wrong. What is the point of therapy if it doesn't make me less autistic? I say nothing, but I want to ask him how I can be myself when he gets so irritated by the things I do.

I want to ask whether he would be OK living with the kind of fear I feel much of the time. I want to know how he would feel if he were incapable of feeding himself three meals a day. I want to know how he would cope with not knowing what emotion he was experiencing. I want to know what it would be like if it took him hours to psych himself up to do something as simple as run a bath. How he would cope when inertia sets in and whole days can be lost sitting on the sofa trying – and failing – to make a slice of toast and butter.

I live with an all-pervading fear of the future. Of what the next five minutes hold. The next five hours, five days, five years. I panic almost hourly about what will happen when the children leave home or how I will cope with growing old in a world that doesn't understand me. Tim just lets life happen around him. I cannot carry on doing this. I have to fight back. It's me against autism and I have to win. Defiance rises in my chest.

We turn into the hotel car park and moonlight fills the interior of the taxi, bathing it in a silvery sheen. I can't read the expression on Tim's face as he pays the driver and then smiles at me. Is it sympathy? I will show him he's wrong. I will show him that I can beat this. This time next year I'll be a different person. Of that I am sure.

I feel a slight chill as I wonder whether he will want to stay the course.

CHAPTER TWO

September 2015

The holiday is over and England feels grey and dreary. I want to hold on to the slightly soporific feeling I get when I'm away but – as is always the case for me – I feel it fizzle out as soon as I enter the arrivals lounge of a British airport.

My head is woolly from the Valium I took to cope with the flight. Flying triggers physical and emotional issues for me. It is rare I can board a plane without experiencing a full-blown meltdown. In the past I have refused to board, gripped by a black panic. On other occasions I have made it to my seat only to find that an additional demand placed on me – the announcement of a delay, an insensitive flight attendant, or a strange noise coming from somewhere inside the aircraft – sends me scrambling for the nearest emergency exit. Usually, but not always, Tim or one of the flight crew eventually manages to talk me down and I slump into my seat and endure the flight in total silence.

The reasons are hard to pin down. Layered over my usual claustrophobia is a sensation of wrongness. Inside the pressurized metal tube, the air tastes different. Sounds are deeper and more painful. My eyes feel dry, my vision blurs, breathing is harder, my centre of balance shifts and I feel dizzy. My heart rate speeds up as I tense against the next sensory assault. Words no longer work in soothing me. Even my special interests bring no comfort.

I turn instead to rituals. It is they that persuade me onto a plane. They are the same each time I fly. As I climb the stairs to the aircraft, I feel compelled to touch one of the metal rivets to the left of the door. I have no idea why I do this. It became a habit more than a decade ago and I feel uncomfortable at the thought of not doing it. The compulsion isn't an OCD-type ritual. I don't believe the plane will crash if I don't do it. Rather, I would just spend the entire flight experiencing a nagging sensation that something had been left undone.

Throughout any flight I have to hold my boarding pass. It remains in my left hand. Permanently. The paper becomes damp, creased. The ink smudges. Putting it down is not an option.

From take-off to landing, I am almost exclusively non-verbal. Speaking feels too hard, so I do it only if I really have to. Questions from the flight crew or offers of drinks or food are met with a shake of my head. Tim stopped trying to engage with me in this context many years ago. Sometimes he'll put his hand on the back of my head or on my knee. I assume he thinks this is reassuring. It isn't, but it would feel unkind to tell him, so I don't.

I'm not afraid of flying in the usual sense. I don't fear a crash. I don't worry the plane will burst into flames or disappear from the radar never to be seen again. I'm not afraid of the aircraft. I'm afraid of myself. Feeling different is so intense that I worry what it might do to me.

The sense of relief I experience when the wheels hit the tarmac and the plane bounces along is immense. Something lifts. If, however, we have to wait on the plane for any length of time before the doors open, I become agitated. Waiting is a painful state, and never more so than when trapped in this way.

As Tim and I wait for the shuttle bus to take us to the car park, I imagine what it will be like next year when I am fixed and can fly without any issues at all. Right now, however, I am consumed by the bad feeling. It's worse each time I have to transition from one situation to another.

The bus stop is crowded. A workman's road drill is torture. A child is crying. The sound reverberates around my head and hurts my ears. There's a siren in the distance. Its insistent scream makes me feel as if I should be doing something to calm it. I'm missing the routine of being away. I want to be sitting by a pool. Reading. Silent.

Even tiny transitions hurt. The change that comes with the end of a weekend makes me feel wobbly and unsure. Monday mornings arrive too quickly and I'm gripped by a sense of apprehension, a tightness in my chest, a feeling of impending doom. There is no logic to it. I know things are no more likely to go wrong on a Monday, but because the weekend offers two days of relative calm – of not seeing or speaking to too many people – the difference is measurable.

Temple Grandin, author of a number of books including *Thinking in Pictures*, once said: *Fear is the main emotion in autism*. That is certainly true for me. Everything new I encounter – even if it is simply the beginning of another week – is seen through the prism of fear. I constantly question what might go wrong: today, tomorrow, next week, in six months. What impact will a decision I make now have on the future? What if I say something wrong to someone, or write something incorrect in an email? What if I forget to pay a bill or don't write the correct time for a meeting in my diary? What if suddenly I'm found out? If people realize that I'm pretending to be something I'm not. A grown-up. A proper person.

There's no instant cure for this fear, but I can distract myself with work and slowly, as I lose myself in writing a feature or get caught up in arranging an interview, it subsides. Little by little until it is at its usual level. The one I have grown comfortable existing alongside. Sometimes I imagine what it must be like not to wear the weight of fear like a winter coat. I wonder if others feel a lightness I will never experience.

I can feel a certain calm on holiday, but the closest I have ever come to experiencing true peace are the seconds before falling under the blanket of a general anaesthetic. I have had a lot of surgery over the past few years and I get through the natural anxiety by remembering that feeling. I've learned to fight against the drugs, to stay with the feeling as long as I can.

It is when I feel most at ease and afterwards it can sustain me for weeks: knowing that it is possible for me to feel unafraid.

Arriving back from holiday, then, feels like Monday morning times a hundred. The long drive home from the airport sees the anxiety increase as the miles are eaten up. I shut down slightly as I watch the landscape whizz by out of the passenger window. I put the radio on, so I don't have to talk. Talking when I'm feeling anxious is exhausting, as if I have to drag each heavy word from my brain to my mouth to form a sentence. What is there to say anyway?

As we reach the final stretch of road before home, Tim is impatient, as if this last bit of the journey is too much to bear. And then we are home. I hear the familiar crunch of gravel under the tyres and count the new molehills that now scar the lawn. There are seven. I scowl at the weeds on the driveway and the sad wisteria over the sitting-room window. I won't relax until I have seen the children and opened the post. But at least I am home.

I get out of the car almost before it has stopped and throw open the front door. The familiar sound of the dogs barking greets me as I scoop up the mail from the table in the hall. Toby is in the kitchen. It's two in the afternoon and he's in his pyjamas eating a bowl of cereal. He hugs me with the awkwardness of a teenage boy as Tim sets our bags down and takes in the empty dishwasher and the pile of dirty dishes in the sink.

The house never feels quite right when I have been away for more than a week. It is somehow slightly surreal. Wrong. Other. As if I have to get to know it again. I have to learn again to accept that the ancient Aga makes a gurgling noise whenever the wind blows. That the kitchen clock ticks with an irritating plasticity. That the rosebush tap-tap-taps against the kitchen window.

The house felt like home before I went away, but that doesn't mean it immediately will when I return. Just because I learned to find some semblance of peace in France doesn't mean I can bring it home with me. When I see Tim or the children after we've been separated for a couple of days, I have to remember how to be with them all over again. They are familiar strangers. It is uncomfortable for all involved and I hate it.

I'm always surprised by how much like men Jack and Toby look. In my mind they are their three-year-old selves, so the fact they are now taller than me and have slightly self-conscious beards is odd. The sink is full, but otherwise the kitchen is surprisingly tidy. It's a relief, but doesn't quiet the uneasy transitioning feeling I'm still coping with.

The boys are in some ways so like Tim and me. Their looks and personalities are juxtaposed, though. Jack looks more like me – with his pointy nose, chiselled bone structure and green eyes – but his personality owes more to Tim. Toby's features are softer and his eyes the exact bright blue of Tim's, but he experiences the world more like me.

When Jack forgets to double-check that all will be OK, he throws himself into life with the exuberance of a puppy. When he remembers to check, he can talk himself out of most opportunities or challenges. He shares Tim's fascination with the physical world, particularly space and physics, but he has also inherited an inconsistent mood that goes up and down in a way I find painful to watch. And he can be distracted and chaotic.

Toby is both of us too, but differently. He can be something of a contradiction. He is measured, and a risk-taker. He likes his life to be structured, but embraces challenges. He likes a degree of sameness and exists mainly on three kinds of food – pizza, pasta and baked potatoes. He prefers things done his way, but is also sociable and capable.

I once heard someone advise the parents of teenagers to get a puppy so someone will always be happy to see them when they come home. It's worked today. Huxley, our springer-Labrador cross, is thrilled to see us. He throws himself at Tim, his fawn-like legs going out at all four angles as he hurls his body towards him. He makes a sound that is something between a bark and a whimper. Conversely, Smudge, our miniature dachshund, wanders around the kitchen; the only clue that he is pleased to have us back is his tail, which is wagging with quiet approval.

The dogs, too, are a perfect reflection of us. Plagued by clinical depression all his adult life, Tim seizes every opportunity that presents itself whenever the black clouds lift for any length of time. Then, he has all of Huxley's boundless energy and enthusiasm. Throwing himself into any adventure without a moment's thought. Kissing the joy as it flies.

I'm more like Smudge, aloof and determined to avoid inclement weather and new situations. Smudge and I like things to be consistent, never changing, and his obsession with tennis balls matches mine with facts.

Toby is now eighteen and on a gap year before going to Goldsmiths to study computer science. He is distracted by something on his phone as he gives us a debrief. What the dogs have eaten, how many times they've been walked, and how much money is left over from what we gave him to cover any expenses. He's been careful, he says, so asks whether he might keep the balance to spend on a new Xbox game. He tells us how he worked out a daily budget to reach this position. I like his exactitude.

Jack, who is in the second year of his gap 'year' and is being assessed for ADHD, stumbles into the kitchen, looking a little dazed, with the awkward, puppy-like beauty that seems to settle on boys in their late teens and early twenties for all too short a time.

'Have you seen my wallet?' he asks before even saying hello. 'I was sure I left it on the table in the hall, but now it's not there.'

There is little to be gained by pointing out that we have been away for ten days and have absolutely no idea where it might be, so Tim and I share a knowing glance and let it go. Jack fills a bowl with bran flakes and adds milk until it is just short of overflowing. When he spoons the first mouthful, milk drips onto the kitchen table creating a puddle that looks like a sheep. He tells us that he spent all the money we left him and had to borrow £20 from his girlfriend, Mary. I'm so thrilled to see them both alive and well and having avoided any trouble that I don't mind at all.

'Can you take me to Zeke's in ten minutes?' Jack asks, chewing loudly. Tim rolls his eyes and inhales deeply as if he's about to say no. He then shakes his head and reluctantly agrees. Toby goes back to his room to download his game.

Jack and Tim leave – arguing only slightly playfully about the selfishness of expecting a lift that will mean Tim will be in the car for another hour, just minutes after getting home – and I am alone. I savour the feeling. The quiet. I take a moment to familiarize myself with the sounds that surround me. The hum of the fridge. The gurgle of the water cooler as it refills. Smudge's snoring. I put the kettle on the Aga, sit down at the kitchen table and light a cigarette. It's warm in here. The boys haven't thought to open a window. I can't be bothered to get up, so stay at the table until the kettle begins to whistle.

I take my case up to my bedroom and begin to unpack. It feels so good to be back in my room. My sanctuary. Tim's bedroom is directly opposite across the hall. People find it odd that we don't share a bedroom and make assumptions about our relationship. We tend to say it's because he snores or is a restless sleeper. The truth is I need my own space. I cannot sleep if there is even the slightest thing to disturb me. I am like the heroine in 'The Princess and the Pea'. I can only sleep if everything is perfectly right. I need crisp, clean linen, soft pillows, an open window and an entire double bed to myself.

The unpacking finished, I dump a pile of laundry in the washing machine and go into our study. It's not pretty but it is functional and the room where words are most easily accessed. There is a white shelf unit filled with scores of books. I have loved reading since early childhood. Some of my favourite memories are based around books. I remember the feeling of freedom when the gates opened at the end of the school day and I begged to go to the library on my way home.

27

There was a whole world contained in those four walls, and it was a world encased in safety.

When I have occasionally been asked to imagine myself in a calm, peaceful space, I don't think of lying on a sandy beach listening to the waves roll in or sitting at the top of a mountain. Instead, I try to conjure up the feeling of being in a London library of the early 1980s.

I don't have a great visual memory, so it won't be a particular building. It will, instead, be an amalgamation of a number. Every library of my memory has common features: parquet flooring, a cool stillness, ladies behind the counter radiating a calm efficiency and pride in a job well done.

Library sounds are my crashing waves. The metal on metal of the date stamp being calibrated, the almost imperceptible squelch when the stamp meets the ink on the sponge, and the dull thud as the date is stamped, indelibly, onto a bookplate. I think of the papery sounds of cards being slipped into indexes, the crackle of microfiche pulled from a drawer, and I feel a sense of calm wash over me. In libraries people whisper. There are no sudden loud sounds, no shouting and no gratingly loud small talk.

I dream one day of recreating a library-like room of my own. Floor-to-ceiling shelves stuffed full of books, all ordered neatly; if not alphabetically then by colour. A conker-coloured wooden floor, where I could sit on a rug and trail my fingers along the edges of the parquetry blocks while reading Enid Blyton, as I did as a small child.

When I think back to my childhood, the memories are always centred around books. The characters within the pages felt more like friends to me than the ponytailed girls I shared a classroom with. I loved Katy Carr, Pippi Longstocking, Heidi, and Darrell from *Malory Towers* far more than the real girls I spent my days locked in school with. The girls in these books made sense to me. They were ultimately good and kind. Some had a bravery, a rule-breaking maverick streak that appealed to me. In real life, rules were never to be broken. The idea of even a minor infraction would send the electric shocks of anxiety shooting through my chest.

I would read those books over and again. When I felt scared, insecure or confused by school life – nauseous at the smell of the food coming from the canteen, hurt and confused by the cruelty of my classmates, or stung with indignation at the sheer lack of logic displayed on a daily basis by my teachers – I would recite passages from my favourite books over and over again in my head.

Even today I enjoy reading a book much more second time around. A first read can be filled with apprehension. What if I don't like the way the story goes? What if something awful happens to a favourite character? What if I get bored halfway through after I've invested something of myself in the story? A second read is a joy. I know exactly what is going to happen, so can immerse myself in the words and the subtleties in a way that would have been too stressful the first time.

A good book can stop my head whirling. It can take me to another world, one where the fear can somehow magically be kept at bay. Books are my greatest pleasure. When the world is too loud, chaotic or confusing for my brain to process, I will go to bed with a book I read when I was a small girl and am still able, at times, to lose myself in the printed text.

Childhood is often a hugely difficult time for autistic people. The rules can be confusing and make little sense. Not being able to choose the clothes you are to wear can be enough to provoke a meltdown. When I was around three I had two identical fun fur jackets. One was yellow, the other blue. My mother talks of how I would happily wear the yellow one, but not the blue.

I can still see myself standing in front of my mother as she takes the blue coat from the cupboard. I am defiant, immovable. She bends down and takes my arm to put it in the sleeve. I begin to scream. I feel itchy and angry. I will not wear this coat. I breathe in and then do not exhale. My mother's expression moves from angry to concerned. My lungs begin to hurt.

My mother is talking to me. I see her lips moving, but cannot hear her words. I am silent. My body stiffens. My lips are tinged with blue. I fall to the floor and lose consciousness.

This happened often during my childhood. My parents were told such episodes were merely tantrums and that they should not give in to them. Three of my own children – particularly Toby – suffered when they were young from reflex anoxic seizures. These are spontaneously reversing short episodes of asystole (heart standstill) triggered by pain, fear or anxiety caused by increased responsiveness of the vagas nerve at the base of the neck. They are utterly terrifying to watch. A child in the grip of one of these seizures will breathe in to cry and not breathe out. They will fall to the ground, stiffen and jerk. It looks and feels as if they will die, but in a matter of moments they are conscious again, often with no memory of what has just happened.

I don't know whether the behaviour I displayed as a child was a seizure that went unrecognized or if our portly, scary GP was correct and I was simply 'engaged in a battle of wills' with my parents.

I cannot imagine I was an easy child. I know I was strange. Grown-ups often talked about me in hushed tones, in a way they didn't seem to about my cousins, classmates or the children of my parents' friends.

It's because she's adopted is a phrase I often heard. Also, She's spoilt. And, She's good at getting her own way, that one. Finally, Maybe she's a bit simple. I only heard this one a few times, but I rather liked it. Simple seemed to me a nice word. It sounded clean and unscratchy.

There were many things said about me, most of which I didn't understand. This irritated me a lot. Not because I cared what people thought. I didn't, but to this day I find it vexing when I can't grasp a concept.

Throughout my entire childhood, however, I never once heard the word *autism*. I don't think my parents or their friends had even heard of the condition, let alone had any understanding of how it related to my odd and eccentric behaviour. It wasn't until the 1988 release of *Rain Man* that autism made its way into the public consciousness. This is somewhat ironic, as the character Raymond Babbitt is based on a man called Kim Peek, who, like Raymond, was a savant, but instead of autism he had FG syndrome, a rare genetic condition.

My own behaviour – the fact I avoided other children, didn't play with toys in the usual way, spoke in a manner well ahead of my years and always had my head in a book – was explained away by the fact I was adopted and was being raised as an only child. Or because I was unhappy due to my adoptive mother suffering from many bouts of ill health and often being hospitalized for long periods.

In north-west London in the 1970s it was seen as important to conform, to behave just like everyone else. I tried so hard to do this – by copying the other girls of my age – but more often than not I failed. I had no idea how to think and feel like everyone else, so instead I tried to look like them, dress like them and – weirdly important to my seven-year-old self – to acquire similar possessions to those they owned. Snoopy was very popular and I liked this because I wanted a dog of my own. Tiny Tears dolls were also fashionable, but they left me cold.

During the long hot summer of 1976, while the country talked of nothing but hosepipe bans, inch-deep baths and how the gardens were suffering, I was obsessing about Ballerina Sindy. I didn't really know why I wanted one, just that everyone who had one seemed happy. Eventually, after much nagging on my part, I became the proud owner of a Sindy doll. I literally had no idea what to do with her. After I had changed her outfit a few times from the carefully arranged lines of matching skirts, dresses and tops, she was relegated to the back of my toy cupboard.

I carefully picked the people I would copy. At school, there was a girl a few years above me. She had long blonde hair that flicked just like Farrah Fawcett's and an air of confidence that seemed to shroud her in a golden light. I found her fascinating. I wanted to know everything about her. I watched her from afar. I don't think she even noticed me. I desperately wanted to know her name.

On the last day of term, when we were allowed to trade our strictly imposed school uniform for home clothes, she came in dressed in cropped jeans, a white Fruit of the Loom T-shirt and a pair of Dunlop Green Flash tennis shoes, on which she'd written 'Elvis' in felt-tip pen. From that moment on she was immortalized in my mind as the Elvis Girl.

She left that term, but for many years when I found myself in a difficult or emotionally draining situation I would consider what the Elvis Girl would do. When school became too much and the older girls screamed insults across the playground, or when I was alone in a room with a boy and knew he was about to kiss me, I would imagine I was her and do what I calculated she would have done. It often worked in calming my fears. I may not have been able to get my hair to flick in the way she did, but I could adopt her inscrutable expression, and power through the pain.

Copying neurotypical behaviour is an exceptionally strong coping mechanism in most autistic girls. Unlike boys with autism, who are often happy to strike out on their own and just be themselves, girls tend to have a strong need to fit in. Mimicking the behaviour, style of speech, interests and social interactions of others provides something akin to a blueprint for life. While neurotypical girls have an innate understanding of how to behave, autistic girls tend to have to learn these behaviours by studying how others do them.

In an effort to add detail to my blueprint for life, I have begun contacting a number of autism experts, including Professor Tony Attwood, author of *The Complete Guide to Asperger's Syndrome*.

He stressed that with autism the core features are generally the same for boys and girls, men and women. There are, however, key differences. He told me: 'One is how girls react to being different. The other is the different expectations in society for girls. In terms of how girls react, I think one of the common ways is to observe, analyse and imitate and create a mask, which delays diagnosis for decades until the wheels fall off.

'What the girl will say is, *I don't get it. I don't understand it, but I will observe it. I will look for patterns.* ASD is a study of patterns. That's why someone with ASD may be so good at maths. Often in ASD you are searching for the patterns of life – looking for patterns in interactions and then analysing them, imitating them and faking them.

'This often means that a teacher, for example, doesn't see the problem because often the girl is a goody-two-shoes at school; she suppresses it until she gets home, where she can be a very different character. What I call "Jekyll and Hyde". Still, she may escape into her imagination, so she is diagnosed with Attention Deficit Disorder.

'But it's often more of an issue in the secondary school years, when socializing is more complicated. Girls can be more bitchy and mean, and Aspie girls don't play that game. They are loyal, trustworthy and kind. They just don't do bitchiness and they find it very hard to understand why girls would actually enjoy being so cruel to each other and so destructive. How could this person be so cruel and vicious to me and then, thirty seconds later, be absolutely nice as pie to someone else? If they were vicious to everyone all the time, you'd get that.

'The other thing is that girls are often expected to be touchy-feely, affectionate, very much engaged in talking about feelings and things like that. So there is a higher expectation of social engagement and empathy.' These expectations can be difficult for girls with ASD.

I was aware from a very young age that not only did I behave differently from the others, but I also thought differently. I read the dictionary for fun and collected words to drop into sentences. I might choose *polemic* as my word of the day and use it as often as I could – unnecessarily, but always in precisely the correct way.

Though I found it physically and mentally exhausting, I think I tried hard to fit in. More often, though, I would create imaginary worlds in my head and would sit still for hours coming up with the rules for this parallel universe. In this new world in my head, the opinions of adults were no more important than those of a child. Mealtimes were optional. Everyone would wear the same clothes every day and they would be made from soft grey fabric that felt good against the skin, not itchy, scratchy or harsh. At school, you could choose what to do. If you didn't like art or PE, you could read instead. Every day the library was stocked with new books. No one shouted or raised their voices. If you ever broke a rule a proper grown-up explained why it was a rule and why it mattered and then you were simply told – kindly – not to do it again.

For years I genuinely believed most of my problems stemmed from the fact I was adopted as an infant and therefore didn't fit in with my new family. In my early twenties I set out to track down my biological mother. I had heard from other adopted people that the process might take years and be a complicated one of considerable forensic detective work. I was rather looking forward to this. I wanted to have a project to occupy my mind, a new obsession. I set about it with typical hyper-focus. It worked. Rather than the work of months or even years, I tracked her down within three hours of being given my birth certificate.

In the UK, those adopted before 1975 must consent to counselling before they are allowed to access any information relating to their adoption. This was frustrating in the extreme; my nature is to want immediate results, but I was forced to agree.

Eventually, on a sunny day in May when I was around twenty-five, I set out to meet Myra, a social worker from Westminster Council. I prepared for the meeting in my usual way. I imagined what the building would be like and telephoned reception to find out whether there was a lift, explaining I would not be able to use it and would need to take the stairs. I studied a map to see how long it would take to get there. By bus from Notting Hill to Paddington would take no more than twenty-five minutes. I allowed myself two hours.

Strangely, in adulthood I have never suffered from social anxiety. As long as I am allowed to be myself, I'm OK. School was forced socialization and *they* wanted me to fit a mould in the quest for homogeneity. Now, I don't care what others think of me.

If that is part of my autism then I am grateful; it has allowed me to function successfully as an adult. I do need to ensure I am not uncomfortable with the practicalities of life – such as being forced to get on the Tube or into a lift – but strangely I can cope easily with many things others might find daunting or scary. My work, for example, calls for me to interview many household names – actors, authors, celebrity chefs and models, amongst others. Perversely, I do this as easily as others might do the weekly shop. Equally perversely, I do not know how to do a successful weekly shop.

The meeting with Myra, however, didn't go quite how I had imagined it. It took place in a soulless room in a drab council building. We sat opposite each other on plastic chairs, a grey Formica table between us. She looked tired and defeated. I had imagined the counselling would be in-depth, that my suitability would be assessed. Was I fit to be given access to the required information? I thought I would be asked questions about my mental health, why I wanted to trace my family and how I would cope.

'You do know that not all parents want to be found, don't you?' Myra said, a brown file of papers resting on her lap.

'Of course. I'm prepared for that,' I replied, wondering if it were true.

'OK, well if you're sure, here's your file. You can't take it, but you can have photocopies of anything you want. They're fifty pence each.'

That was it. She then left me alone in the room for fifteen minutes. I opened the file and came face to face with my past.

My adoptive parents had been advised to explain to me very early on how I came to be with them. They made it into a story and, as I grew up, it became just a fact, something that made me slightly different from other children, but not something loaded with emotion. I didn't feel the sharp sting of rejection other adopted people talk about. I don't think it damaged me in any way.

For as long as I can remember I'd had a list of facts about my adoption. Facts make for comfort. My natural mother's name was Marina. I had originally been called Samantha. I had some siblings, although no one knew how many or whether they were boys or girls. I knew that my mother had been *on the stage*, a phrase which now seems hilariously outdated. I knew I was born in London, at St Mary's Hospital in Paddington, and that my mother had been unmarried. This last fact made grown-ups wince a little, as if it somehow diminished me. I could never quite work out why.

New information jumped out at me. Marina had been married long before she had me, to an American wallpaper designer. She had lived with him in New York. She had four children with her husband. Boys. She had come back to England alone, leaving her husband and children behind. She had been in her early thirties when she had me. I had imagined her as a teenage mother.

There were letters from Marina to the adoption agency, so I got to see her handwriting for the first time. It was round and neat; not at all like mine. She explained a little about her life, both in relation to my adoption but also adding what she described as background information. Some of it was surprising. While I had imagined her stage career had been as an actress, I was intrigued to learn that she had, in fact, been an underwater ballerina with a show that toured the country. From the descriptions in one of the letters, it would seem as if she had at some point danced in a tank with crocodiles.

I also discovered that I had been born Catholic. This surprised me; my original religion was something never discussed at home. My adoptive parents were Jewish, so perhaps this mixture of genetics and environment contributed to my extraordinary ability to hang on to guilt.

Jewish north-west London was a tiny place in the 1970s. It wasn't just that everyone knew everyone; it was that everyone knew what everyone else was doing. Where they were going, whom they were seeing, what arguments or romances had broken out. Who was dieting, who was putting on weight. Whose marriage was going through a rough patch. In fact, pretty much everything up to and including exactly what everyone else was thinking.

Almost everything was also done in a group. My parents worried that I, as an only child, would be lonely, so friends and cousins were rolled out at every opportunity. I have two sets of cousins: Alison and Karen, who are five and ten years older than me respectively, and Jacqui and Paul. She is two years older and he two years younger than me. I adored my female cousins. Paul less so; he was noisy and threw things.

I didn't connect in the way I now know others do. I was clingy and followed the girls around. Being older, they had their own concerns and their own secrets. I remember clearly sitting on Alison's bed while she and Karen talked in code over my head. Fingers tracing the pattern on the pale yellow candlewick bedspread, I tried to work out what the encrypted conversation meant. I knew beyond doubt it was exciting.

These days we think we live in a world where information is exchanged immediately, but nothing today goes viral as quickly as a drama that happened back then, in a world before mobile phones. One mistake or slip-up and you felt the eyes of an entire community boring into you.

Our mothers seemed to have a sixth sense that allowed them to see into our heads and pluck out information that told them if we had misbehaved. It was a close community. It was loud, passionate and full of crisis and hyperbole. I found it utterly overwhelming. My need for space and calm was completely at odds with a world where people could turn anything into an argument. They seemed to feel slighted by the strangest of things. Receiving news second-hand, for example, was a no-no and met with the kind of reaction more worthy of a punch in the face.

Try as I might, I couldn't understand the emotional outpourings or the absence of logic or perspective. Now, with the benefit of age and experience, I can see there was nothing inherently worrying in these displays of emotion, but at the time they were confusing, bewildering and unnerving.

Jewish life in the 1970s did have one thing that worked for me: routine. Friday nights in particular. I liked the clockwork nature of Shabbat eve. As the sun went down my mother would light two candles and say a prayer. It was a calming ritual and one I looked forward to throughout the week.

Friday night supper was always the same in every Jewish house I visited. Chicken soup with noodles and strange half-formed eggs, and dumplings made from matzos. Roast chicken followed, with potatoes and vegetables. Challah, a sweet-tasting bread made with egg, would be blessed and eaten with a little salt, and then thick, sweet red wine – usually Palwin No. 10 – had its turn to be prayed over before we were all allowed to take a small sip. From my earliest years my definition of a sip was questionable.

Often after supper we would go to synagogue as a family. We drove. To do so was against Jewish law, but then so was the bacon my father sometimes ate when not at home. It worried me such rules were being broken. I didn't believe there was a god that would punish us, but what if I was wrong?

I was always slightly afraid of the synagogue as a child. The men took it in turns to stand guard outside and I was frightened of the nameless thing they were protecting us from.

On a wall inside, a plaque talked about the death of six million people in the Holocaust. I didn't know what this was, but I did know it was somehow relevant to the sentries outside.

Mostly, however, I found time in the synagogue intensely boring. There were, of course, words, but these were in another language, one whose fancy letters I struggled to make out. I would distract myself by reciting as much of the Hebrew alphabet as I could remember. Alef, Bet, Gimel, Dalet . . .

I would long for the service to be over. Afterwards, people would stand around in the car park talking, the conversation often loaded with emotion, voices rising and falling. Exchanges I couldn't understand. I think this is why I eventually moved to the country, as it is quiet, both indoors and out.

My office at home could not be further from the organized library space of my daydreams. I try hard to keep some kind of order, but it is full of paper that seems to multiply on a daily basis. I cannot tame the flow. I don't know how to keep on top of it. Am I meant to keep my electricity bills and, if I am, for how long? Is it really necessary to keep paid parking fines from 1996? I can only deal with things like this if I have been explicitly taught how.

Tim – too arty for the mundane and unable to commit to staying on top of the direct debits, the children's UCAS forms or insurance renewals – is happy that my insistence on being in control means I will not allow him to handle such things. In his hands I am sure we would be plunged into chaos. Despite this, I fear every single task. What if I accidentally put an extra zero on a number on a direct debit form? What happens if I get my bank account number wrong? *What happens?* It's the start of so many of the conversations I have with myself.

Today, I go through my Sunday routine as I have every week since I can remember. I paint my toenails, wash my bed linen and then look at my diary for the week. It always feels as if I won't be able to complete the tasks listed or make all the journeys planned. I have to try to imagine what each day will be like so there are no surprises. Good or bad. I make no distinction between the two.

I sit at the kitchen table. Shabby and warm, it's the room where my family wanders in and out looking for lost earphones, books and wallets. Where they come to ask for appointments to be made or cancelled. To complain about the speed of the broadband. To ask for lifts from one end of Norfolk to the other. This room holds my fondest memories of when my children were small and has been the backdrop for the whole of their lives.

It's here they have announced late in the evening that they need to go to school the next morning dressed as dinosaurs. It's here they have sobbed over tricky homework and broken hearts. And it's here that Tim and I have had all our important conversations. It's a cliché, but our kitchen is the epicentre of the house and I cannot imagine what it will be like once the children have gone.

I look in my diary. I have an appointment with a therapist on Thursday. It has been set up by Dr Somayya Kajee, the psychiatrist who first diagnosed my autism. I am nervous. I have had therapy before, but have always felt as if I were somehow doing it wrong. Choosing the right therapist is rather like choosing the right boyfriend and I have placed all my trust in Somayya having found the right one. I need this to work. It feels like my last hope. I need things to change and this therapy needs to deliver.

The new therapist – whom I will simply call M – will probably want to talk about my childhood. Others enjoy reminiscing about penny sweets, bad pop songs and TV programmes they spent hours watching. I do not. I don't view this period of my life with any great affection. Most of the time I felt that appalling prickly-on-the-inside sensation that you get just before you cry.

I feel I must prepare. Should M ask me questions about childhood I want to be able to answer them accurately. There's a cupboard in my office where we keep the important things:

tax returns, passports, birth certificates. At the back, on a high shelf, is my childhood photo album. I take it down and the dust I disturb makes me itch. It was put up there when we moved in more than sixteen years ago and hasn't been touched since.

Back in the kitchen, I wipe down the red plastic cover and feel my heart rate rise as I open it. The pictures start when I am around seven months old. I can't feel anything for the baby in the black-and-white photographs. She is as alien to me as a random stranger. I age progressively. I am four and wearing red shorts and a white T-shirt. I am seven in a blue dress with a swirly pattern. I am ten and in my smart school uniform.

I try to feel something. Anything. I want to tell the child in saturated Kodachrome that I understand why she is the way she is. I want to tell her it isn't her fault. Isn't our fault. Isn't anybody's fault. That it will be OK in the end. I want to tell myself that too. Here and now.

I'm drawn to the period detail. The television with its spindly legs, which, throughout my childhood, looked old-fashioned but now looks rather stylish. The drinks cabinet with curly carved wooden legs throws up interesting memories. As a child I would sit underneath it for hours, with Fluffy, my toy rabbit, and a book. I liked to imagine it was a machine that could transport me to the world within the pages.

In one photograph I'm tucked up in bed, cradling a hot-water bottle. Chickenpox. The doctor had just been. His name was Dr Newman and, even as a young child, I could feel his air of superiority. When he said of each new symptom that it was 'just one of those things', I wanted to ask why. What does 'one of those things' mean?

I've learned over the years that patients with complicated conditions, like EDS, often feel like this when faced with one doctor after another. I am not, though, sure that many feel it as early as five years old. Dr Newman was an odd-looking man. He slightly resembled Winston Churchill, but his hair was sparse and dark and oiled down onto his head. There were gaps where his pink scalp peeked through and it made me feel a little sick to look at it. His hands were huge and his fingers fat, like sausages.

Medicines were a big part of my childhood. There was the pink one for earache, the white one for tummy ache, the chewable Junior Aspirin, the orange one for sore throats, and Phenergan for just about everything else. For anything external there was witch hazel in its brown glass bottle with vertical lines that felt nice under my fingertips, and the pungently scented pink Germolene.

Then there were the pills my mother took. I remember knowing early on that medicine split into two categories: good and bad. Sore throat medicine was good but the pills my mother took for her 'nerves' were bad. She was often ill. She took a lot of pills. Thinking about that time, I feel a huge sadness. For her. For me. For my father. I also remember knowing beyond doubt that to get by you had to show no weakness and allow no one to discover the strange things that went on in your head.

I push my chair back from the kitchen table and stretch. Huxley, on the kitchen floor next to me, follows suit. Looking back is painful, so I do what I do when trying to process complicated emotions: I send myself back to that place. I lean forward and hit the keys on my laptop . . .

Big School – Autumn 1975

I am in the school playground. The ground is hot and feels sticky under my new black Start-rite shoes. Shoes have to be either Clarks or Start-rite as these are good for your feet. The pretty shoes at the cheap shoe shop are not good for your feet, so you can't wear them.

I like my new shoes because they are shiny, but I don't like them because they are hard. They are nice to look at, but not to wear. I have to have white knee-length socks. They twist around and fall down. I don't like my socks. They are not good socks.

I have been at this school for three weeks and two days. It makes me sad. I want to be back at Mrs Hadar's kindergarten. I liked it there. We had cold milk and biscuits at ten o'clock every morning and a nap in soft blankets every afternoon.

There was a garden at Mrs Hadar's with a sandpit. The sand was different to the kind you get at the seaside. The grains were smaller and softer and I liked to let it run through my fingers. Sometimes the other children would annoy me by playing messily with the sand, getting it wet with water, and being noisy while I just wanted to touch the sand in quiet.

I am not allowed to go back to Mrs Hadar's. Another girl, Emma, is allowed to because she has a brother and sometimes, like on Christmas shopping day, she is allowed to go with her mummy to collect him. Her brother is horrible. He isn't nice and isn't clean. But maybe it would be OK to have a brother if it means you can go back to Mrs Hadar's.

Mostly I am sad now. I can't play with Geoffrey anymore. Geoffrey is Mrs Hadar's sausage dog. He is golden brown and has a nice red collar. I always draw a picture of Geoffrey on Fridays when it is drawing time. I am bad at drawing, so I do not have a nice picture of Geoffrey. This makes me feel sad too. When I grow up I am going to have a sausage dog and I am going to call him Claire and give him a pink collar. Mrs Hadar told me you can't call a boy dog Claire, but I think maybe you can, if you're a grown-up and you give him a pink collar.

I like things to be pink. At Mrs Hadar's I was allowed to wear pink ballet shoes. Only they weren't called ballet shoes, they were called slippers. I think this is because you can't wear them when you go outside. At school you have indoor shoes and outdoor shoes. The indoor shoes are called plimsolls. I don't like them because they smell horrible. Mummy says this smell is called chemical.

We will have to go into the classroom soon. When the bell rings. Teachers take it in turns to ring the bell. It is bad to be standing next to the teacher who is ringing the bell because it is loud and it hurts your ears. I don't want to go inside. The room is hot and it smells horrid. I think it is because of the milk, which sits by the window and gets all hot. I am told I am naughty because I won't drink the milk, but I can't because it is warm and it tastes funny. Mummy says I must try, but I don't want to.

School is very big. It's much bigger than Mrs Hadar's, which was just like an ordinary house. We go in through the side entrance because children are not allowed to go in the front. I don't know why. There is one very big building and the new block, which is smaller, and some mobiles. The mobiles are my worst rooms because the floors wobble when you walk on them and I get scared the mobile might fall over.

Today we are going to be making a collage. It will be on one big piece of paper and everyone on my table will have to stick things on. Working with the other children is hard because they do it wrong. I am in Panda Class. A panda is a black and white bear that lives in China. Next year I will be in Neptune, which is a planet. It is the furthest from the sun and seventeen times bigger than Earth, but Pluto is my favourite because it is the smallest and it has five moons, not one like the Earth. After that I don't know what class I will be in and this makes me sad because I like to know what is going to happen.

There are lots of children in the playground now and we have to line up to go into school. We have to stand in pairs and hold hands. I don't like holding hands and I don't have a special friend, so Mrs Everett chooses a partner for me.

I don't want a partner and don't see why I have to have one. I have to hold Francine's hand, which feels slippery and wet. I would like to be at the end of the crocodile on my own. Or I could be at the front, but not in the middle because that feels squashy and like I can't breathe.

In the classroom we have to listen to a story. I can't concentrate on the story because we are sitting on the floor and the carpet is itchy. It's not like the carpet at home. It is made of green squares and if something gets spilled on it and it can't be cleaned up, then a new square is put in. I think the old, unwanted squares are lucky because they don't have to be in school anymore. I can't sit still because of the carpet and it is making Mrs Everett look at me a lot. When she looks at me I don't know if she is cross or not, so I make sure I never look at her and then it's like she can't see me.

It will be playtime soon. I don't enjoy playtime because I don't know what to do. Some of the girls play games, like one of them being the mummy and the others being the children. I don't want to do this. I tell them I think it's boring because it is.

Mrs Everett told me that we have to go into the playground every day to play even when it is snowing, but if it is really heavy rain we can stay indoors. Every day I hope it rains.

I want to stay in my classroom and not go and play in the playground but that is not allowed. Sometimes I sit on a bench and read a book. I am reading *What Katy Did*. It's about a girl learning to be good. I have read it three times. Some of the children in my class can't read very well and some can't read at all. They are called slow and might have to go in a different class if they can't learn. I won't get moved to the slow class because I am clever. I might get moved up a year, though, as Mrs Everett tells me I am not being stretched enough. I don't want to be stretched. I think it might hurt. If I do move up a class maybe I will be able to take Fluffy.

I would like to bring Fluffy to school because he is a good friend. Fluffy is my favourite toy, but Mummy and Daddy say I will lose him and I will scream. He is a white rabbit. I am allowed to take Sheena, a pink and cream bear with orange plastic eyes. She is my second favourite toy. I think Mummy and Daddy think I would not scream as much if I lost Sheena.

After playtime we have to go back into the classroom and

play with the sand. It isn't as nice as the sand at Mrs Hadar's. It is hard and scratchy and there is not very much room for all the children. I don't want to play like this, so I sit in my chair. Mrs Everett is pulling a face and tells me this is naughty and I must do what everyone else is doing.

I look at the clock and see that it is a whole hour until lunchtime. I don't want to stand at the sandpit for an hour. It makes me feel dizzy and hot. I watch the second hand of the clock go round and round and count every second from one to sixty. I have to do this sixty times but it is OK because I am good at counting. I can do everything they ask us to do at school, but I don't tell them that because there are some things I don't want to do. I never put my hand up because it hurts and it makes me feel strange to be talking out loud in front of the whole class.

When I am on my own with grown-ups I am called a chatterbox, but when I am at school I am called quiet. I am a quiet chatterbox. Sometimes I say this in my head. Quiet chatterbox. Quiet chatterbox. Quiet chatterbox. I like that there are lots of T sounds and if you say the words really quickly in your head they sound like a train and sometimes in my head I add choo choo at the end. Quiet chatterbox. Quiet chatterbox. Quiet chatterbox. Choo choo.

After the sandpit there is lunchtime. This is the worst part of the day. School food is bad because it is grey and slimy. I don't know exactly what some of the food is called and I don't need to know because I will never ask for it. Anywhere. The worst is the mashed potato. It is lumpy and has bits in it that are like string. They don't put it on your plate with a spoon. They use an ice-cream scoop. This is really stupid as ice-cream scoops are for ice cream. Today it is mashed potato and meat pie. The meat is in a sauce that is like jelly. For pudding there is semolina with jam in the middle, which is disgusting. All the food is soft. I like food you can crunch. Like crisps and carrots and chips.

The dinner ladies give me food that tastes so horrible it

actually makes me feel sick. You get into trouble if you don't eat the food, but I just can't. Even the smell in the canteen makes me want to be sick. I keep asking if I can bring a packed lunch like some of the other children. I am not allowed though. I don't know why and it isn't fair.

When I sit in the canteen I feel a prickly feeling inside. I don't want to eat the food. It feels funny in my mouth and then my chest feels like it is moving upwards and my mouth won't chew even when I try very hard to make it. I don't think different foods should touch each other but the dinner ladies won't help when I ask for things to be away from each other.

Today I don't eat lunch and get told to stand in the corner of the playground until the lunch break is over. I like this because I am alone, but I don't like it because it makes me feel hot and wobbly and like I might fall over.

Just before lunchtime ends, Mrs Everett takes me into the classroom to have a talk about food. She asks me why I won't eat it and I tell her it is because it is disgusting. She tells me that this is a rude thing to say. I don't think it's rude, I think it's true. She asks me if I like school and I say I don't like it because it is stupid and not like Mrs Hadar's. Mrs Everett tells me I am spoilt and might have to go to see Mrs Sturdy, the headmistress, and tell her this.

Mrs Sturdy is the boss of the school and if she knows that the food is bad she might be able to change it for me. She also might be able to get better sand and cold milk. I tell Mrs Everett I would like to go and see Mrs Sturdy and this makes her sigh. I once asked my friend Hazel why grown-ups make that noise. She said it is called a sigh and people do it when they don't like something or are a bit cross. I still don't know why grown-ups sigh or what it means. When I ask them they sigh more and that makes it even more confusing.

There are many people at school who tell lies and I would like Mrs Sturdy to know this because telling lies is a bad thing to do and she can make them stop. Every time someone lies I write it in my notebook. I write about everything in my notebook. I am a good writer – much better than other children of my age.

Sometimes I write about the other children. I wrote that Katherine is the nicest. She is in my class. She is very pretty and has good hair, which is never knotted. My hair is long and is often tangled. I hate having it brushed. I am taller than Katherine and much thinner. I wish I looked more like Katherine and less like me.

Mark is the most horrible. Sometimes he says bad things to me, like saying that my mummy is mental.

'Your mum's a nutter and so are you,' he said, with his face too close to mine. I don't know what this means and I don't want to ask him because he makes me scared. When he said this the other children, boys and girls, laughed. I think Katherine also laughed and that made me most sad. My notebook is my most important thing – after Fluffy – and I would be very upset if it got lost.

I don't like Mrs Everett because she makes me do things I don't want to do. But I also don't like her because she tells lies. She lied when she said I would have a nice time at school. I am not having a nice time.

Everyone at school lies, but when I tell them they are lying I am the one who gets into trouble. It's not fair.

The dinner ladies lied when they said the food is yummy. The food tastes horrible. Annalisa lied in assembly when she said she was going to be on an advert on television. I haven't seen her on an advert so I think this is a lie.

The lady in lost property lied too. She said that my jumper would turn up and it hasn't. I think someone else took it home, which makes me want to go to everyone's house and have a look until I can find it. I hate my jumper, but even more I hate that it is in the wrong house. Things should be where they are meant to be and it makes my head feel funny when they are not.

All the children come back from lunch and we listen to poems. There is one called 'The Big Rock Candy Mountains'.

I quite like it, but the best poems are in *The Cat in the Hat* and *Green Eggs and Ham*. People like to read *Green Eggs and Ham* to me because they say I am a fussy eater. That means I am like Sam, who does not like green eggs and ham. Like Sam I am.

That rhymes and I like that because I like poems. We have to write them. Today we have to write a poem about weather. This is my poem:

> Silver and sparkling
> Snowflakes fall
> The world is like
> A fluffy ball.
> All around
> The world is white
> What a lovely
> Pretty sight.

In class, Mrs Everett reads some of the poems out. Mine is the best. I have to stand at the front while Mrs Everett reads it. I hide my face behind my hand because all the children are looking at me.

After we have read poems, it is time for PE. I hate PE. We have to wear our vests and knickers. In front of everyone. It is wrong. Knickers are private and I won't get undressed in front of other people. I scream when they try and make me do this. Lots of the girls don't like showing their knickers, but I am the only one who screams. Today I try really, really hard not to but I can feel hot tears behind my eyes and I think I might scream.

After school I go home with Alison and that is OK. She is my cousin. She is in the Juniors and I am in Infants. This means that even though we go to the same school I never see her there because our playtimes and lunchtimes are different and infants are never allowed to cross the playground line into Juniors. It is called out of bounds and it is very naughty to go anywhere called out of bounds.

I like Alison's house and I especially like her bedroom because it is always very tidy without her even trying. I get muddled in my bedroom, so it is always messy and this makes me feel confused about where things are. I like things to be lined up neatly. All my toys are in a line in my room, but sometimes I am not very good at putting my clothes away, so they are on the floor and I get into trouble for this.

Tidying up is hard. Harder than reading or writing and much harder than doing sums or watching *Lizzie Dripping* on television. I like to know exactly where everything of mine is and get very upset and cross if I can't find it. I do not like it when I can't find something and it makes me have what Daddy calls a tantrum.

Because Alison is older than me, sometimes I am allowed to walk to the sweet shop with her. It is my favourite place to go. It smells lovely as if all the sweets have got together and created the best smell in the world. In the shop there are two types of sweets. Those that come in jars and have to be weighed by Mr Ellington and ones in packets that you pick up yourself and take to the counter.

In the jars, I like the pink shrimps, milk bottles and the sugar mice that have string for a tail. I only like the pink ones though. Not the yellow or white because they don't look or taste as good.

In packets, I like Treats, Mint Cracknel (which I think tastes like minty glass), Milky Bar and Munchies. These are much more chocolate than sweets, but I don't like packet sweets because they are things like Opal Fruits, which are the wrong kind of sticky and taste a bit like plastic. Alison is allowed Golden Nuggets because she is older. It's like bubble gum, which I am not allowed in case I choke on it. Alison told me that if you swallow bubble gum it stays in your tummy forever.

I eat the food at Alison's house. Her mummy makes biscuits every day and we sit at the table and eat them. I love having lunch there as there are lots of different things to choose from and there are always chives. I like chives. Eating them is like eating grass that tastes nice. Proper grass doesn't taste nice. I know because I have tasted it to see if it is like chives. It is not like chives.

Daddy is going to pick me up later when he has finished work. This means it will be after my bedtime. I will have a sleep at Alison's house, in the spare room, and then I will go home in my nightdress. I am not happy when this happens because I hate waking up when I am asleep. Being asleep is the best part of the day and it isn't very nice when I have to wake up.

Fluffy will be at home, though, waiting on my bed. That is the good bit. It is easier to go to sleep when I am at home and Fluffy is there because I like things to be in the right place and the right place for me to be asleep is in my own bed.

I often have to have a sleep at Alison's house or at Hazel's house across the road. Hazel's house is quite nice because there is a conservatory and she has a cat. It is a quiet house because Hazel's children are grown up and this is nice for me because it means I don't have to put my fingers in my ears.

There are lots of plants in Hazel's house and the floor is made from wood which has a pattern like some I see when we do easy maths at school. Hazel said it is called parquetry. She showed me how to spell the word and I was surprised there was Q for queen instead of K for king as it sounds like it should be spelled *parkertree*. When I go to Hazel's house I usually sit in the conservatory, which is at the back, but sometimes I am allowed to read in the sitting room, which is at the front. Then I can look out of the window and see the cars going by.

One day a lady came to my house after I had gone to bed and gave me Sheena. The lady said she was a social worker. She came to make sure everything was all right because I am adopted. This means that a lady had a baby that she didn't want because she was on a stage and she wanted to do that and not be a mummy. So she gave me to my mummy and daddy because they couldn't have a baby of their own.

The social lady was nice. She asked me questions like

what do I like to eat and am I happy at school. I said that I like to eat chicken and roast potatoes and that school isn't nice because the food is bad and the teachers aren't very clever. Then I was sent back to bed so she could talk to Daddy.

Mummy wasn't there because she was in hospital. The lady asked me if I was sad about this, but I was not. I don't think about Mummy when she isn't there. I don't think about anyone when they are not there.

Mummy has something wrong with her called nerves. Nerves is a bad thing to have. It's not like when you get chickenpox or a sore throat and everyone is kind to you. When you have nerves it makes people cross and they shout. They don't give you hot Ribena or rosehip syrup and you don't get sweets and books. I hope I don't catch nerves, because I don't want people to shout at me. When they do I sometimes scream or go very, very quiet. It's like hiding in the airing cupboard where no one can find you.

Sometimes I look at other mummies and see if there is one I would like more instead. I think I would like Katherine's mummy because she always smells like a garden and has nice clothes and she hasn't got nerves.

CHAPTER THREE

November 2015

I meet my new therapist, M, in Norwich, in the same offices where I had my autism assessment. It's an elegant Georgian building with high ceilings and rooms that look as if they were designed for entertaining. The one we are in now is reassuringly exact and has a black fireplace with a white surround. Above it is a framed seascape. The walls and carpet are the same pale green. I have real problems with this colour. Overall, though, the room has an air of calm and quiet, as does M.

I look at her and try to make sense of what I see. I find it impossible to guess her age. I can't do that with anyone. If I were forced to, I'd say early thirties, but I could be out by as much as ten years.

She is wearing a blue cardigan, a sensible maroon wool dress, and boots. Her clothes are functional, but I can't help thinking she must be uncomfortable in them. I can almost feel the scratchiness of the dress around the neckline and wonder how she copes with tight cardigan sleeves over a dress. I would hate the feeling of the sleeves not being completely level with each other. The thought makes me squirm a little in my seat. I want to pull the dress sleeves down. M's boots make a tiny squeaking sound as they rub together when she crosses her legs.

Her face is clean of make-up and her light brown hair is cut in a bob. Her skin is pale and unblemished, her eyes intelligent and concerned. She smiles easily and has a manner that suggests she is entirely comfortable with herself. I hope she has someone to tell her how lovely she is.

I imagine her life. I'm sure there are children and that they are quite young. I'm sure there's a husband too. In my head, he is quite serious and has a job where he also does some good in the world. I make up stories for everyone I meet. Knitting together words in my head makes the person more real to me and somehow less scary.

M and I sit facing each other. She shuffles through some papers on her lap. I am never comfortable being the one who is not in control of a situation. I think I have a habit of 'interviewing' everyone I come across, but am fully aware this would cross the boundaries. I've had the kind of therapy you see on American TV, where the therapist says nothing and an uncomfortable silence hangs in the air. I wonder if M really is shuffling papers or if she is waiting for me to reveal something big about myself.

When it comes to silence, I always break first. Usually with a joke.

'You use humour to hide from your problems,' a therapist once said to me before asking me to choose which cushion I would like to play the role of my mother. I laughed and, once I started, I couldn't stop. Turns out Gestalt therapy was not for me.

M won't be asking me to tell inanimate objects that they screwed up my life because they wouldn't let me play the clarinet when I was seven. Her specialism is Cognitive Analytical Therapy (CAT) and she is used to working with autistic people. This helps me feel more comfortable. CAT is like a cross between CBT – Cognitive Behavioural Therapy – and something more analytical that looks at how and why you feel the way you do, based on past experiences. It is designed to provide coping strategies.

Once M has located the piece of paper she's looking for, she smiles warmly and I know in an instant that this time the sessions with her will offer so much more than anything I've experienced in therapy before.

'Is the temperature OK in here for you?' she asks.

I say it's fine and that I am quite warm enough without

being too warm. If I am too hot or too cold, I can't think straight and it is likely – if I don't leave the room – to bring on a meltdown.

'Is the chair comfortable?' she asks. 'Not too bright in here for you?' M is obviously well versed in the sensory issues of autism.

I feel looked after and like it. Usually if a room is in some way making me feel bad, I don't say anything. I find a reason to leave or suffer in silence. The consequence would be that the experience, whatever it was, would be diminished. I wouldn't be able to concentrate, only able to think about getting out as quickly as possible.

There are boundaries in therapy that I want to respect, so I don't intend to go into huge detail about what happened during each session, or about M herself, as she values her privacy. Instead, I'll concentrate on what I learned.

'What would you say your main issues are?' M leans forward in her chair and crosses her hands in her lap, waiting for my answer.

'I have made a list,' I say and proceed to work through it. 'Number one on my list is I want to feel less frightened all the time. Number two is that I want to find a way to organize myself better. I feel as if I've always missed the milestones everyone meets and I want to begin trying to catch up. I'm terrified of committing to anything, so want to learn to do that. I want my relationships to feel better. I want to learn to feel instead of think. I want to learn how to do all the normal things people do, like manage their money, remember to eat, have friends, be organized. I want to know what I like and what I don't. I want to stop being so confused by the world. I want it all to be easier.'

M gives me homework. She asks me to watch a TED Talk on vulnerability by Brené Brown. She gives me a *feelings wheel* to take away and colour in. I'm struck by the sheer number of feelings shown. I just don't feel any of them. Apart from fear. What does *responsive* feel like? *Valued*? Or *insignificant*? How can anyone feel insignificant when they are at the centre of their own life experience? It all seems so complicated and confusing to me. M also asks me to keep an anxiety diary and to bring it back the following week.

Tony Attwood believes autism and a degree of anxiety are, sadly, common bedfellows. 'I'm trying to seriously think if I've met someone with Asperger's for whom anxiety was not an issue,' he tells me. 'It's hard to find one. I think there are neurological and psychological reasons why the rate of anxiety is so high. When I talk to adults with Asperger's in groups – sometimes several hundred – I will say, *OK, guys, what are your biggest challenges?* Most of them say managing anxiety and they say it affects their quality of life far more than any other ASD feature.

'One [neurotypical] approach is to say to the person with Asperger's that they should just relax. The person with Asperger's says, *I don't know how to relax.* Neurotypicals just switch on relax. The person with Asperger's can't find the switch. It's like trying to fall asleep – the more you try to fall asleep, the more elusive it is.'

Dr Somayya Kajee, the psychiatrist who diagnosed me at the Anchor Psychiatry Group in Norwich, agrees that anxiety may be a factor of autism for many. When we talked about it, she said: 'I think autistic people have anxieties generally and they have anxieties about a lot of things. Diagnostically, when we look at co-morbidities, we look for what they have in addition to what is presented as a symptom of their autism. Do they have a social anxiety as well, or OCD?'

I asked her whether people with autism experience anxiety differently.

'It's really hard to disentangle it. Any person – and those with autism are individuals – experiences anxiety in different ways. I suppose that's where we make sense of it for the individual.

'When I saw you I said you have some of these rigidities, but I felt this was very much in keeping with your autism, rather than your having OCD. We spoke about how it was that you can do what you do and still have autism. But again it is about expectation – you get anxious if things are not what you expected or are not going how you planned.

'So I felt it would be explained by the autism rather than, say, a separate social anxiety, which we do see. It is really important I think to tease out those differences. But even if you did have social anxiety, the treatment of that social anxiety would be very different to how you would treat the anxiety in somebody who didn't have autism.'

I also spoke to Dr Jessica Eccles, a lecturer in psychiatry at Sussex University, where she has spent the last three years looking at the relationship between hypermobility – which is a core feature of EDS – and psychiatric symptoms, including work in a neuro-behavioural/neuro-developmental clinic. She believes anxiety in those with autism may also be influenced by an altered interpretation of physical sensations. She told me: 'There is a strong association between autism and anxiety. It particularly seems to be physical anxiety. Some of that may be to do with awareness of internal bodily sensations and bodily focus.

'It's called interoception. My colleague, Dr Sarah Garfinkel, is doing some work showing that in people with autism, hypermobility or both there is a mismatch between the subjective experience of their own internal bodily sensations and how accurate they are at interpreting them.'

Talking to M is easy, but I am aware this is my first therapy session and it will possibly get a lot harder. I have never quite found that breakthrough point others talk about with therapy. I have never found it painful and have never become emotional. I think maybe this only happens in movies or I've been doing it wrong, or it happens for people who have buried past pains deep in their subconscious. I am here to learn how to fix my life. I am here to work hard. I listen intently as M explains how to fill in the anxiety diary.

I have to record the date and detail the feeling, the point I recognized I was feeling anxious, how I responded, how those around me responded and the effect it had on me. I can do this. It is essentially compiling facts, something I am good at.

Later, at home, I resolve to start the diary tomorrow but look at the feelings wheel, determined to colour in something. The boiler has run out of oil again, so we have no heating. I choose the feeling *cold* and colour it in with a grey pencil. I'm wondering, though, if a different kind of cold is meant here. I also colour in *scared*. In red. Red seems the right colour for the feeling of being scared. I feel it exactly as I did as a child. I am most scared of getting something wrong, doing something bad, being in trouble.

I felt it when I was very young, but it grew so much stronger once I got to high school. Teenage years are hard for most of us, but throw autism into the mix and it gets so much more confusing. At the very time we are learning about ourselves, we suddenly have to confront the fact we are different from most of our peers.

The girls at school seemed to have had a secret briefing that informed them of exactly how to behave. When they huddled together in the playground, the conversations bounced without missing a beat from boys to cherry mint lip-gloss. From future careers as fashion designers, journalists, models or something in TV to upcoming exams and parties at the weekend. They touched each other easily, too, applying mascara to each other's lashes, creating intricate French plaits, linking arms as they walked across the playground, and hugging when someone was in tears over a failed romance or an impossible exam question.

They spent their weekends at each other's houses in Laura Ashley bedrooms, listening to mix tapes on portable stereos in neon pink or custard yellow. They recorded the Top 40 from the radio religiously every week and edited out the songs they didn't like. They bought albums and taped them for each other, practised calligraphy until they had decorated their school rough books with intricate black, swirly writing more appropriate for a historical document or wedding invitation.

I wanted so much to be part of that and, although I did sometimes get invited along, I was never quite in the middle of a group. I was always on the edge, always getting it slightly wrong, never quite feeling part of things. I was on the outside looking in on these female friendship groups. I was the last to be called when a party was being planned or some incredible gossip was available to be shared, an afterthought. I didn't have that one special friend the others seemed to. I drifted in and out. I wasn't hated, but I wasn't loved.

One of the things school taught me is that although most grown-ups tell you they want you to be truthful, they don't. They want a sanitized version of the truth. One that has been nicely cleaned up. One that works for them. They don't want you to lie outright about where you have been and what you have been doing, but they also don't want the unfiltered truth that exists within the minds of teens, or other adults, come to that.

Once, in an English class, we were asked to write the story of our parents' first meeting. We were meant to go home and interview them. The others wrote stories of parents meeting at dances, in offices, at the homes of friends, at university. Some stories were deadly dull. Some were sweet and others downright funny. The boys fared worst and, when asked to read them aloud, they blushed and shuffled around on the spot. They spoke to their shoes and the rest of us could barely hear.

I forgot to interview my parents, so wrote my piece on the way to school, sitting on a bench in the park I would cut through on my walk. The frost on the wood was stinging the backs of my bare legs. Instead of writing about my adoptive parents, I wrote about my biological parents, the ones who had brought me into the world.

> You had the temerity
> To ask to make love to me

On a rug by the fire
As we lay
You lied to the liar
Later, sated,
You wrapped yourself
In my oatmeal linen sheet
You offered conversation
I declined.

They didn't know what to make of me at school and I
didn't know how to make it right. I tried so hard to fit in and
be what the teachers wanted me to be, but each time I flunked
an assignment it took me further away somehow.

Things could have been different had I gone to a school
which understood autism. Sarah Wild is head teacher of
Limpsfield Grange, a residential school in Surrey for girls with
communication and interaction difficulties, including autism.

When I told her the story of my poem and the lack of
understanding with which it was met, she said: 'That's such a
shame – it's a really creative response to an open question. One
of the gifts of being on the spectrum is that the connections
you can make are totally different. If you're neurotypical and
interested, they're mind-blowing. Often I can't even see what
leaps someone has taken to get to that point.

'When you look at it from this perspective, you can start
seeing autism as an advantage, because we need people to
think differently otherwise we'll never make any evolutionary
leaps. Sometimes people on the spectrum can think so far outside the box that it's really important.'

I'm not sure I was ever praised at school for thinking differently and didn't have a strong sense of belonging. Being
raised as Jewish helped somewhat; we were expected to stay
within our religious group and not exclude anyone within it.
Our parents knew each other well. They tried to ensure no girl
was left out.

There was a casual anti-Semitism at my school, which occasionally bubbled up and became nasty. Swastikas were drawn on people's lockers, along with anti-Semitic slogans. Fights broke out between the Jewish and non-Jewish boys. There was always a sense that something worse might happen, but it didn't. It simmered under the surface and it was what forced the girls to include me.

I was envious of the girls who bridged the gap between the Jews and the non-Jews. Debbie was most successful at this. She was tiny and incredibly cute in a naughty way. She said the things no one else dared to; to teachers, to bullies, to boys. She looked a bit like Kylie Minogue. At twenty she moved to Australia and has been there ever since.

Debbie had a quality I longed for. She was fearless and she was never bullied. I used to think this was because she had an older sister at our school, but I realize now it was because she simply wouldn't allow anyone to put her in that position. She would show from the off that she couldn't be intimidated. She was too hard a challenge. The bully would wander off and find an easier target. Someone like me.

I had my group of friends, but there was always a barrier between us. We couldn't connect. I knew it was my fault. Even when I briefly had a best friend, Natasha, it didn't work out. She was too needy for me. I felt subsumed by her, drowned out and confused by the intensity of what she wanted from me. She expected me to spend all my free time with her and didn't like it if I saw any of the other girls alone.

She thought we should have lunch together every day and walk to and from school together. She expected us to spend Saturday nights together and to sleep over at each other's house, not leaving until just before bedtime on Sunday evening. I needed much more alone time than is usual for a teenage girl. She needed no time alone. We were both only children and yet we had completely conflicting needs.

She became jealous if I spent time with anyone else and would try to start arguments. I found it frightening and confusing. She was bright and funny, though, and we could sit in her bedroom and giggle about nothing for hours. Once we went to see the film *Endless Love* and her mother misheard the title, thinking it was called *In This Glove*. We found it hilarious. We laughed for a week.

We would pore over teen magazines like *Patches*. We'd watch *Top of the Pops*. She was sure she was going to marry George Michael. I wasn't sure marriage was for me. I fantasized about living alone, although even then I didn't think it would ever be possible. We'd paint each other's nails and try to concoct reasons why our parents should give us extra freedoms. We became close when we were twelve and by Natasha's thirteenth birthday we were allowed to go out together until 8 p.m., as long as one of our parents picked us up.

By the time we were fourteen we had more or less gone our separate ways. I occasionally went to under-eighteen nights at clubs like Busby's on Charing Cross Road and the Wag Club in Wardour Street, which I found loud and overwhelming and quite dull, as it transpired I didn't really understand how to dance.

The other girls from school were less needy and, although often I felt I didn't quite fit with them, I never felt consumed in the way I had with Natasha, who would frequently storm off in a huff for no obvious reason. I missed her, though, and we became friends again later, although the friendship followed a similar pattern and once again we fell out. The divorce from my first husband clashed with her wedding and she felt I was somehow trying to steal her thunder. For years I believed it was all my fault. In hindsight, I can see it was a clash of needs; mine to have space and hers to feel connected.

Teenage life was difficult in so many ways. Our days were mapped out for us and there was no respite. School, activities, homework, food – everything – had to be crammed into the waking hours, which back then were between 7.30 a.m. and 9 p.m. Where was the time for me to daydream, to think, to read and to be alone? When could I just be me? I like set routines, but I need to be in control of them. Then, I was required to go from one thing I hated to the next. Being unable to understand my emotions, I wouldn't recognize when I was becoming overwhelmed, when I was close to burnout or melting or shutting down.

When I was fourteen my parents got a dog. It was a cross-breed, rescued from a shelter. It was named Brandy, which made me wince every time I had to say it out loud. But he was at least five years old, so it seemed unfair to foist another name on him. He smelled dreadful, made weird snuffling noises and was aggressive to strangers, but he gave me the perfect escape. Whenever I needed to be alone in my thoughts I was able to walk him. I would pull on my Converse high-tops, pop on my Walkman headphones, grab the lead, call the dog, slam the front door and walk out into my own world.

I have always had intense interests. They could be described as obsessions, but many autistic people feel this is a negative word with bad connotations. They prefer the term *special interests*. I don't mind *obsessions* – it's how they can feel to me, all consuming. Others have suffered at the hands of professionals who have tried to curb their special interests and stop them from taking refuge in them. So I can see why it is contentious.

My teenage special interests included Audrey Hepburn films, dog breeds, clothes, make-up and books. Reading has been a lifelong special interest. In a good week I can read at least four books. In my teenage years I could read from the moment I got up to the minute I went to bed. I would find somewhere cosy to sit and not move until my book was finished. I would forget to eat or drink, I would ignore the phone if it rang, I would forget about the homework I was meant to be doing. Everything would drift away and it would be just me and the words on the page.

Autistic special interests are often also a safety net. Being able to escape into something we love protects us from the harsh and confusing outside world. In girls, these interests are often not that different from those of their peers. It's important to note that it isn't the subject that's unusual, it's the fervour with which the interest is pursued. I read the same books as the other girls, but also more obscure titles. I went through a phase of reading everything Nancy Mitford had written, even though her books were not fashionable at the time.

The obsession peaked when I discovered Jilly Cooper's books. Lots of my friends read them too. They didn't, though, read the same one twenty times over, beginning again as soon as they finished. They couldn't name every character and answer questions that would stump a *Mastermind* contestant.

Special interests generally cause more problems for those around them than for the autistic person. I talked of little else to my friends than the plot of Jilly's latest book and could argue for hours about their literary merit and why they shouldn't be called bonkbusters. My friends read them and then passed them on to someone else in our group. I could never even contemplate lending one of them and still, more than thirty years on, I know exactly where every copy is in my house.

I like to read books about people who inhabit a landscape I understand. Most of the fiction I read is set in England and the characters live lives not dissimilar to mine. I read them because I am fascinated by people, but need the context of a world I understand. A book set in Iran or Syria would take me too far out of my comfort zone and I would find it challenging rather than cushioning. I don't like books where people suffer in a realistic way, or where there are real world problems that have no understandable solution. I need to know that all will work out OK in the end. I read a lot of self-improvement books too, hoping to find a way to fix the things in my life I find overwhelming. So far I have never managed to stick to a plan.

In my teens I would sit outside cafes on the King's Road or in Hampstead flicking through the latest Jilly Cooper release, devouring every word. Not just because they were thrilling, pacey and addictive, but because I thought they offered a blueprint for how people behaved. I genuinely believed that if I could just be more like a Jilly Cooper character, I would be a normal person.

Sitting at a table on the pavement – usually with hair moussed into curled perfection and wearing my favourite stripy, three-quarter-length trousers and an oversized white T-shirt – I tried to learn how to behave around other people. How not to be seen as odd. I genuinely read Jilly Cooper as you would read an instruction manual for a washing machine. I thought I would find all the answers to life within those pages.

Jilly taught me about human behaviour, but she also taught me to appreciate poetry and to use it as a balm when things are uncertain. Since reading *Rivals*, in which one of the characters works on a biography of W. B. Yeats, I have often escaped into the yellowing pages of a favourite anthology of poetry whenever I have felt overwhelmed by confusing emotions.

For Tony Attwood, this special interest is evidence of someone trying to learn how to navigate her world. He told me: 'This is you trying to understand people, and what I find in girls – in comparison to boys – is that they are much more intelligent and creative in trying to resolve the challenges they face.

'That can include the use of imagination. Sometimes it's science fiction, sometimes it's witches and wizards. Sometimes it's being a journalist. Sometimes it's being a person who has an appreciation and knowledge, for example, of Shakespeare, who understands the nature of Shakespeare and becomes an academic in that area.'

Like many teenage girls I obsessed about love. I was enchanted by a broody, moody boy who seemed only intermittently to notice my existence. He had everything I then believed a boy should have. Irish roots, blue eyes with long lashes, a sneer that could make one freeze and a detachment that acted like catnip to my teenage self. He was The Boy.

I would spend hours getting ready to casually bump into

him. We'd go back to his house, where he would studiously ignore me while we sat on his bed listening to Bob Dylan or Pink Floyd. I would eventually uncurl myself from where I had been sitting, my leg brushing against his, and then wander downstairs to make milky instant coffee for us both. Invariably his mother would be in the kitchen, sitting at a shiny, circular, white table, reading a novel. I adored her and I think she felt a kindness for me that was rooted in the knowledge that The Boy, her only child, had this devastating effect on me.

If I close my eyes I can imagine myself back there, cradling a mug of steaming Nescafé, gazing at The Boy and quickly looking away if he happened to glance in my direction. His room was big, with leafy William Morris wallpaper and the lingering scent of half-smoked joints. His TV was always on with the sound muted. We would lie on the bed together, but not together, not touching, almost pretending the other wasn't there, gazing at the screen while loud music played.

We watched Margaret Thatcher, her head always slightly tilted, striking miners and their exhausted wives. Riot-weary policemen, shiny game show hosts in colourful suits. We watched families eating supper, ads for gravy granules shot in a kitchen not unlike the one downstairs. Glitzy American soaps and sometimes things that made no sense at all as they were silently relayed into the room to a backdrop of Dylan, The Doors, and Hendrix.

An hour before my father was due to pick me up, I would begin to count down the minutes, glancing obsessively at my chunky pink watch. My eyes would go from TV screen, to my watch, to The Boy. I would will him to kiss me. I believed that if I thought about it hard enough it would somehow pop up in his head and he would lean over, take my face in his hands, and his mouth would find mine.

More often than not he would instead languidly half fall off the bed to grab a textbook and lazily recite Latin verbs. I am not good at reading people, and to this day I have no idea if he was ever aware of my longing.

Once, we went to France on a whim. Me, him and a few other boys. We bought a cheap camera and took pictures of ourselves in rural train stations as we tried to find our way to Le Touquet. After too much wine, sunshine and laughing, he leaned over and kissed my cheek. Whoever was holding the camera snapped at just that moment and the picture made its way into my teenage diary, along with the train tickets and the ring pull from a can of French lemonade he bought me.

Had The Boy ever asked me out, things would have been very different. I would have freaked out. The evenings in his bedroom were as much as I could cope with. I got comfortable with the feeling of longing, but if that feeling had been reciprocated I would have panicked hard.

It's a pattern I have repeated through my life. Notice someone or something. Believe I want it. Pursue it. Land it. Enjoy the feeling of having it for a moment. Panic. Panic. Panic. It is an all-consuming fear. When I am heading for a relationship, a new job, parenthood, gym membership, a new friendship, or anything that requires commitment I feel as if I may somehow become subsumed. That my life will be somehow forever changed. That I will have to stop being the whole me and instead become part of something else.

Tony Attwood recognizes this behaviour. He tells me: 'Girls can sometimes make friends but not keep them, because of the intensity problem. Because either she hardly ever contacts her friend or she sends her twenty texts a day and, when the friendship ends, she feels betrayed and can be very black and white in her thinking.

'The other side of the coin is when someone seems too intense to the girl with autism. This is why I see autism almost splitting into two groups. There's the extrovert intense, what I call the Italian drivers. They don't read the signals and they get upset because it's not working. And there are the introverted, withdrawn, shy types. In other words, it's the person choosing solitude or being alone, or being highly motivated to socialize, but very upset when it doesn't work.'

The fear ahead of any commitment comes, I think, from an all-consuming worry that, whatever this new thing is coming into my life, it will stop me from being able to pursue my special interests. It will take up too much space in my head. That it will add a new layer of somebody else's routine into my life. That it will be jagged and jarring and will want more than I am able to give.

I have felt this in every relationship I have ever had. Emotions fall into only two camps: the ones that feel good and the ones that feel bad. Mainly they stay in their rightful places, attached, and don't move. Thinking about money feels bad. Reading books feels good. In the case of relationships they can veer from making me feel good to making me feel bad. Other people are so confusing, so again I strive for neutral.

Yesterday I googled The Boy and got nothing. He has disappeared into thin air. Then later, when I couldn't sleep, I wondered if somehow I had imagined him. I messaged an old friend from that time and asked if she knew what had become of him.

'God knows,' she replied. 'And good riddance. He was trouble.'

I don't believe autistic girls and women deliberately seek out 'bad boys', but I do think we might not be as equipped as neurotypical women when it comes to spotting men who might let us down or reading the signs of a relationship.

I asked Tony Attwood. He confirmed that Aspies often lack the insight needed to make sound decisions about relationships.

'People with Asperger's,' he said, 'are often not very good at character judgement. They don't spot predators. My concern is the high level of date-rape Aspie women experience and abusive relationships. In part it's because of low self-esteem and not realizing that this person's character is actually toxic.'

I asked him if it could also be because we don't quite understand what love should feel like, and so confuse it with other things, such as drama. Or that we come across a boy who seems in pain and we want to make it better, without realizing that this is not the basis for love.

He said: 'Yes, girls may think, *I can fix him. I can make him better*. As you say, they see it as him having a problem, but that's all right. They'll fix it. Realizing they can't and that this isn't a healthy relationship is not something they'll often recognize for themselves. It often comes from those helping them or from other Aspie women, who will say, *I've been in some terrible situations, please don't follow my path.*'

I recognize so much of myself in his words. I know I take people at face value and am unable to read between the lines, so will become close to individuals others would run a mile from. I have often wondered if I experience love in a way that is different from others.

Tony Attwood believes this may be so. 'Another emotion that needs to be explored and understood is love,' he told me. 'What is it? Do people with Asperger's understand and express it in the way that neurotypicals expect? Neurotypicals will have an expectation of how love should be expressed and that may be difficult for the person with Asperger's. I think of it as love languages. Often love by someone with Asperger's is expressed through practical deeds rather than words and gestures of affection.'

I'm often surprised when a situation spins out of control. I have begun many relationships with men that I understood to be completely platonic, later to discover that they read things very differently. I can be intense at the start of a friendship. I love to learn new things and new people may have knowledge and experiences I haven't come across before. I get excited about new facts and that excitement can be contagious.

My social style is easy, fun, and, above all else, different. I have learned that men can find this attractive and confusing. I'm a quick communicator. I can't easily leave a text or email or call unanswered. I perhaps seem more intensely involved in the friendship than I actually am.

This leads to a mismatch in expectations. I think we're exploring a new friendship, one I naturally imagine will be doomed to failure. He, on the other hand, will often imagine this intensity is the sign of something more. I have been caught out by this a number of times. Tim often warns me when he sees it coming. He calls each of them my *latest scrape*.

I am, though, subconsciously hungry for more social interaction than I naturally have in my life. It is always at a slightly superficial level. Because I find neurotypical women slightly frightening, most new relationships I form tend to be with men. They are easier to read and more straightforward. They don't feel slighted by my directness or my inability to commit to plans. I think that because of this I have often in the past ignored Tim's warnings.

As for The Boy, I think he had a lot of issues and didn't have the emotional maturity to know how to treat any girl, let alone one like me. Nothing ever happened between us, but he remained my obsession for four or five years. Even now I can be transported back to those days by a Jam song playing on the radio or the sight of a red, vintage rugby shirt.

Looking back now, I believe that by obsessing about someone unsuitable I protected myself from having to have a real relationship and having to deal with all the confusion that that would have brought with it. I had the odd boyfriend, but they rarely lasted.

Would I like to go back to my teenage years, knowing what I know now? God, yes! A million times yes! I would love to do it all again with the knowledge of my autism and the skills I have built up in the intervening years. Would I want to experience again the same emotions I did then? I'm not sure. I find emotions – my own and other people's – scary and overwhelming.

On an intellectual level I understand that getting close to someone is a scary experience that will invariably lead to doubts and fears, but being aware of the other person's feelings can be truly bewildering.

When I talk to Tim about this he says: 'I think you're *autistically* missing the point. Most people find getting close to someone can be exciting, intimate, unique, warm, reassuring, companionable, safe, secure, precious and so on. The point is, you don't and I'd love to understand why.'

I want to give him an answer, but I don't know how. Why are some people scared of spiders and others unmoved?

The Boy, I think, was also a useful distraction from the torment that was school. I was impossible to teach. I had scraped through primary school, which was quite progressive and focused more on creativity than exams. At high school I couldn't learn the things they were trying to teach me. I would sit in a class looking at equations on the blackboard that simply made no sense to me. They were a different language, one not recognized by the operating system that drives my autism.

My brain would cloud over when slides of water tables appeared on the screen in geography and I would struggle to understand even the most basic maths. English was OK. I enjoyed the reading side of it and I liked writing, but I couldn't grasp the basics of grammar and spelling, with which I still struggle.

I went to a sprawling and chaotic comprehensive school, a forbidding red-brick building with a central hub and huts that looked as if they were made from cardboard peppering the grounds. It was the backdrop to an assault on my senses for eight hours each day. The collective hum of children's voices multiplied and became a large bassy rumble I could feel in my chest. The sound of school chairs scraping against the floor and desk lids slamming was magnified and felt like an act of violence. I had a plummy accent. One that stood out. I spoke differently from the other girls and that – and my weird behaviour – made others not in my friendship group suspicious of me.

There was little outright hostility; they just avoided contact or wouldn't choose me for a team. When we did spend time together the atmosphere seemed scratchier, less comfortable. There were more misunderstandings and a feeling that we all wanted the encounter to be over quickly.

My primary school had been cosy and cosseting. I didn't make friends, but I really didn't mind. We were always being assigned partners or put into groups for activities, so I don't think the teachers really noticed. At break times I would sit alone reading a book. If a teacher tried to get me to join in with the skipping games, I would find an excuse not to. I thought everyone saw life as an obstacle course to be carefully navigated.

High school held new terrors every day. It was then that I realized not everyone experienced the world in the same way as me. It was my first understanding of cognitive dissonance. I was more intelligent than most of my classmates, so why could I not understand the work being set for me? My exercise books were a mess. Ink smudged with tears of frustration and sweat from my fingers as I tried to make sense of the problem laid out in the accompanying textbook.

While I didn't learn much at school, it was during my teenage years I learned about hiding my differences and blending in. I would watch girls and copy their mannerisms closely. The way they dressed, the music they listened to, the magazines they read. I would study their likes and dislikes and try to make them my own. I'm not sure, when I look back, what was authentically me and what was borrowed.

Teenage Me – Summer 1984

We've spent much of the summer on the King's Road, my friends and me – sometimes in a big group, at other times in pairs. Sometimes I come here alone. These are my favourite times. I like that I can do what I want and I don't need to think about talking. I can look in the shops I want to, or I can drink milky coffee at a table on the street while reading a book. I think I like books more than people.

There are two reasons we spend time here. Everyone is completely enchanted by the 1960s and for some reason they all think most of the decade happened roughly halfway between Sloane Square and World's End. I want to know why they think this, but don't want to look stupid by asking, so I don't.

I think it has something to do with Mick Jagger and, possibly, a lion. I'm not sure whether the lion was actually with Mick Jagger, or whether one or both of them lived on the King's Road. To be totally honest, I'm a little bit hazy about who Mick Jagger is, although I do think he's been in a band, or maybe a film.

The second reason is My Old Dutch. It is, everyone agrees, the best restaurant in all of London and on a good day we manage to eat two whole pancakes each. One savoury; one sweet. I always have cheese and mushroom and then maple syrup and ice cream.

I find food difficult, which annoys my parents a lot. My friends talk about it too and I know they think I'm anorexic. I went to the library and got a book called *Solitaire*, which is written by an anorexic girl. I don't recognize myself in her description, but I know I can only eat food I really like, which is why pancakes are good. Sometimes we go to Maxwell's for burgers or Pizza Hut for pizza, which I like less. Sometimes the food feels funny in my mouth and I have to spit it into a tissue. Sometimes people see me do it and I know they talk about me afterwards.

At home I hide food in tissues or take margarine tubs to the table, so I can put food in them when my parents aren't looking. Mummy made me go to see Dr Newman to talk about food and not eating. He said she should try to let me eat what I want. I tell her I want to be a vegetarian, but I still eat meat when I am out.

This summer there has been a restlessness, an impatience.

Not necessarily a sense that something is about to happen; more a feeling of desperation that it will and a fear that it might not. I think we all feel it a bit, maybe except Sheryl, who seems so much like a proper grown-up. We never talk about it, though, and the feeling isn't given a name.

We are fifteen, at least most of us are. Claire is sixteen and this – plus the fact that she has an eighteen-year-old brother called Jono, who looks like an actor – makes her the de facto leader of our group.

Claire's house, which is two bus rides away (we are scattered across London), is one of our favourite places to be. Having put in eighteen years, her parents now seem tired of child rearing and are longing for an empty nest. Buoyed by the success of having kept one child alive to legal adulthood, they have a seriously laid-back attitude to rearing the younger ones. So laid-back they have moved to the top floor of the four-storey townhouse, locked the door and rarely come down.

They are unusual parents, more concerned with each other than with their children. They seem genuinely in love, something Claire finds mildly disgusting and the rest of us rather intriguing.

The father, Paul, endlessly paints the mother, Viv, often with her naked and draped across a chaise longue. This means she has to spend a lot of time 'sitting' for him, which in turn means she is rarely around to keep an eye on us.

We spend most of our time in a semi-derelict orangery in the garden. Many of the windowpanes are either missing or broken, but the glass still intact is thin, almost like sugar glass, and the cream wrought-iron mouldings are intricate and beautiful.

'Majestic in its ruin,' Lara says one day. 'It is the epitome of faded grandeur.'

'And there was me thinking it was just our smoking den,' Claire laughs, taking a packet of Sobranie Cocktail cigarettes out of the back pocket of her jeans.

Liv sits down on the orangery floor, puts a cigarette in her mouth and lights a match. She is wearing a sugary pink lipstick, which leaves a stain on the filter. She puffs valiantly, but the cigarette has lit unevenly and is burning faster along one side.

Lara rolls her eyes. 'Give it to me,' she says, leaning over and plucking it from Liv's mouth.

Lara relights it and hands it back to Liv and takes one for herself before offering the packet around. The golden tips glint in the light. One cigarette is turned the wrong way round, and I reach to take it when my turn comes.

'Not that one, Laura,' Liv shrieks. 'That's my lucky one.'

I pick up the box of matches and light first Lara's, then Amanda's and then go to light my own.

'Stop! It's unlucky to have the third light,' Amanda squeals.

The criticism stings. I feel a sharp pain at the back of my throat and tears coming. I swallow hard and draw on the cigarette. Will I ever get the hang of the rules everyone else seems to just instinctively know?

The others are coughing a bit, but that doesn't happen to me. I love it. It is as if my lungs have been waiting for this moment forever. The acrid taste and slight kick at the back of my throat feel welcome and strangely familiar. Maybe it was being driven to Cornwall in my parents' car with them chain-smoking, the windows tightly shut.

Jono's girlfriend, Sylvie, wanders in barefoot, wearing one of his shirts. Her long legs are silky and brown. She is heaven and I so want to be her. At eighteen, her glamour is as unattainable to me as that of a movie star. She is holding a bottle of Malibu. She takes a swig, wipes her mouth with the back of her hand, and passes the bottle to Claire.

'Want some?'

Claire drinks from it and smiles. 'Malibu always reminds me of Ibiza.'

The bottle makes its way round and finally it is my turn. I take a large gulp and feel warmth spread through my veins.

'Hey, don't down it in one,' Sylvie laughs, but kindly. 'It can take a bit of getting used to.'

The burning taste of coconut still in my mouth, I pass the bottle on to Liv and sit with my eyes closed, the sun hot on my bare legs. Sylvie is talking, but her words wash over me.

'Jono's taking me to Crazy Larry's tonight,' she says. 'But Ben's going to be there so I don't know if I really want to go.'

The bottle returns to me and I take another mouthful. This time, I hang on to it and take a second swig. Sylvie is still talking.

'Last week he took ten ounces of hash with him and kept trying to rope us into helping him sell it.'

I'm feeling floaty and there is nothing in my mind but the sun and Sylvie's slightly thin, flat voice. She bends over me.

'Look, Laura's asleep,' she says, her long curly hair tickling my nose. She reaches over and takes a blanket from a bench and begins to tuck it under me.

It is a perfect moment.

No pain, no fear, no worrying about doing or saying the right thing. No thoughts of home or school, or The Boy, or being in trouble. Just the dappled sunshine and the feeling of nothingness.

CHAPTER FOUR

November 2015

'Who in your life supports you?' M asks at our second therapy session. We're in a different room today. It's larger, grander. There's a partners' desk at one end and the room looks like a film version of a lawyer's office. M has pulled two chairs into the middle of the room and we sit facing each other.

I think hard about the question. What does it feel like to be supported? I suppose one's husband should be supportive, but what if I'm not able to allow anyone to do this for me? What if I am just not cut out for marriage and, if that's the case, why have I married twice?

I married for the first time when I was just twenty – to Michael, a couple of days after his twenty-second birthday. We were children, although we didn't think so at the time. I was certainly too young and, looking back, I married for all the wrong reasons. I thought it would fix me or make me complete. I had failed at school and failed to settle into a job. I was too scared to travel, ill equipped and unqualified for university. I had no idea what I could do with my life. Marriage seemed like a good option. Surely that was something I could succeed at?

A few months before the wedding, I had panicked and had tried to call it off. My parents were horrified. The invitations had gone out. Hats had been bought. And so, on that hot August day, I walked down the aisle hoping against hope that this was the thing that would save me.

The day after the ceremony we left for our honeymoon. We would be spending three weeks travelling through France, alone together. I didn't feel old enough. Part of me almost expected a grown-up to say they needed to accompany us.

As soon as we arrived in Paris, I spun out. I had found out a week or so before the wedding that I was pregnant and the moment we checked into our hotel my morning sickness began. I spent the first night of our honeymoon in a Parisian hospital. I was terrified. I couldn't speak French. I was vomiting violently and had terrible pains in my stomach. I thought I would lose the baby.

I didn't feel connected to Michael. I felt alone and on the other side of something impenetrable. I think it was the first time I realized that feeling isolated while with someone is the worst kind of loneliness.

We left France soon after this, cutting our honeymoon short. I hated being away from home. I couldn't cope with all the changes being sprung on me at once. I was married. I was pregnant. I was ill. I retreated into myself and allowed myself to be swallowed into a typically autistic shutdown.

On arriving back in London I was immediately admitted to hospital for three months. I couldn't stop throwing up. I hated the ever-present nausea, the dashes to the loo, the feeling of acid in my throat, the fear that I would be eroded by it.

More than this, I hated feeling different. I had stopped feeling like me. I still have this with any illness, even the mildest of colds. I cannot tolerate feeling anything other than my usual self. Illness – even simply a blocked nose or sore throat – causes me to feel uncomfortable. It is as if I no longer quite recognize myself.

Awash with hormones in a small room in a London hospital, my focus narrowed to the space between the bed and the loo, unable to move any further than the tube on the saline drip would allow me to. The room was overwhelmingly brown, a colour I find hard to cope with at the best of times. The carpet was the kind of nylon that squeaks beneath one's feet. Everything in the room was made from a material that grated. I was trapped in this tiny brown cell. I was a child about to have a child.

The Boy came to visit. Sitting on a brown plastic chair, he draped his legs on the hospital bed and ate the grapes someone had brought. He lit a Marlboro Red. The smoke rose and hung around the ceiling. I tried to tell him of my fears.

'I think I'm in hell,' I told him, looking down at my fingers, which were folding pleats into the bed sheet.

'It was hell in Da Nang,' he said, adopting a fake American accent. Vietnam war films were big around this time.

Part of me had hoped he would rescue me from the bed I had made for myself. I have spent many years since longing for someone to rescue me. Every time things become too hard I dream of a knight on a white charger, someone more equipped for life than I am, to make it all somehow OK.

Instead, The Boy told me he was off to travel the world. It was a pattern that year. Friends dropped into my hospital room carrying backpacks, telling me they were off inter-railing through Europe or going to America, to the Far East, to India. Everyone was leaving.

Michael came to visit. He couldn't have been nicer. Every day he'd tell me how things would get better, how the sickness would pass, how we would be a family. I hadn't really allowed myself to think that far ahead. Hadn't allowed the idea of me becoming three to permeate my brain. I was stuck in the moment, trying to hold on.

My mother-in-law, whom I adored and who was one of the main reasons I believed I could cope with marriage (she did it so well), dropped in with some new nightwear for me. I was shocked when I looked at the label. It said *age 12*. Struggling out of bed and looking in the mirror, it became clear just how much weight I had lost. My cheekbones, always pronounced, now pushed at my raw skin like the wrong fingers in a glove. My ribs were visible. My hipbones sharp and pointy. Sitting on a hard chair hurt as there was no flesh padding out my bottom. I was physically and mentally being steadily erased.

Weeks later, I found myself alone in our tiny flat. Michael

was at work and I moved from one room to the next, imagining what it would be like doing this with a tiny baby. I don't think I was depressed, but my mood veered between melancholy, fear and guilt. Michael deserved a better wife and my baby certainly deserved a better mother.

The forty weeks passed quickly. I went into labour violently. There was blood, lots of blood. I was haemorrhaging. I was panicking. Michael was panicking. An ambulance was called. My GP, who lived in the same block of flats, came down and told me it would be fine. It didn't feel fine as I looked down at the puddle of thick red growing larger on the white tiles of the kitchen floor.

I don't remember much about the labour, apart from at one point willing myself through it by thinking that – at the end, when it was all over – it would be as exciting as getting a new kitten.

When the moment came and I met my daughter for the first time, everything else fell away. I felt consumed with love. She smelled so delicious I had a primal urge to lick her. I looked into her eyes and clearly understood for the first time what love feels like. We called her Lucie. I thought I could make it work. I thought I could stay married and be part of this new family with a tiny baby at its centre, whom I loved more than life itself. It wasn't to be.

M coughs quietly. She is looking at me intently.

'How is your relationship with Tim since your diagnosis?' she asks.

I'm meant to be working on how I feel now, but all I can do is think back on all the mistakes I have made. It is as if I have to catalogue each of them in my head before I am able to move forward. The guilt is overwhelming.

'Where did you meet?' M asks, trying a different tack and switching on a lamp on the table next to her.

It's a question all married couples have a story for. We have two. The truth and the lie.

Whenever the question surfaces, Tim and I hesitate for a

moment, before one of us will say, 'We met through a friend. Tim was sharing a flat with her while he was going through his divorce.'

This version of events is the lie. The truth is that we met at the Charter Nightingale Hospital on Lisson Grove in Marylebone. I was twenty-three and being treated for a benzodiazepine addiction. Tim, nine years older, was being treated for depression. I was still married to Michael and Tim had just separated from his first wife. Like me, he was adopted, but it had left him with issues of rejection he believed may have contributed to his depression.

Though I didn't know it then, my EDS was at the heart of my health issues and it was what led me to be admitted to the Charter. Pretty much every woman I have come across with Ehlers-Danlos syndrome has, at some point, been misdiagnosed. Often it is with chronic fatigue or fibromyalgia. If they are one of the many who is also autistic, they might have been given a diagnosis of bipolar disorder, borderline personality disorder or even Munchausen's.

I got off fairly lightly. I was misdiagnosed with hyperventilation syndrome. I got my diagnosis from a doctor recommended by a family friend. He gave me a prescription for some seemingly innocuous blue pills. I took them for eighteen months and, although I still had pains in my joints, episodes of fear and a feeling that all was not right in my body and brain, things were calmer. I did feel a little better.

I was desperate for Lucie to have a sibling. I didn't want her to be an only child like me. I wanted so much to become pregnant again. After months of trying, I went to see a doctor, who found a problem. I had a small operation and within six weeks I was pregnant with my second child.

I was pleased, but things weren't brilliant between Michael and me. I was struggling to share a small space and my life with someone else. I became secretive, retreating into my head, not being able to talk about how I felt.

Lucie and I were inseparable, though. I understood this

small person more than any other human I had ever encountered and I was pleased that soon she would have a new sibling.

A few weeks before I was about to give birth to her sister (I had found out her gender as soon as possible – I don't like surprises) my obstetrician retired and I had to start over with another. Doctors frighten me. It's easier now I have my autism diagnosis. I feel I can be honest, tell them I'm scared, and explain why I find consultations difficult. Before, I had no explanation, it felt like another failure on my part.

My new consultant was the scariest kind. In his early forties, he was suave and busy. His consultations were quicker than I was used to and the examinations made me feel uncomfortable. I filled in a form before I saw him for the first time and one of the questions was about regular medications. I listed Lorazepam.

He told me I'd have to stop taking the pills before I had my baby, that they were dangerous for her. Why had no one else told me? He suggested I be induced three weeks after our first appointment. I was terrified. Anything medical made me panic at the time, but I had no idea of what was to come.

I stopped taking the pills forty-eight hours before I was due to be induced. I felt jittery and scared. I couldn't eat or sleep. My pulse raced. I had a pain in my chest that felt so wrong. I looked in the mirror and my face seemed different. I knew I was going to die, or go insane, or die, or go insane. I knew this couldn't be normal. I rang the maternity ward in a panic. They said they would track down my consultant. He rang me at 11.30 p.m. and told me to hang on, that it was OK.

I can't remember much about the birth of my second daughter, but the feeling of love when I saw her was just the same as it had been with Lucie. We called her Tatiana, later shortened by almost everyone to Tatti. Immediately I knew she was her own person. I thought all babies were the same, but on meeting her, I knew she'd be an adventurer.

Lucie came in with Michael to visit her new sister. A doctor was in my room doing a heel prick test on Tatti. She was screaming. Lucie took in the scene and began to cry. She breathed in and didn't exhale. We waited. Her body stiffened, her back arched. Michael put her down on the bed. The young doctor looked concerned. I was frantic. He couldn't find a pulse. A team rushed in. There was talk of meningitis. They whisked her away to another ward. Michael went with her.

I struggled out of bed, unable to stand up straight, in pain from the eighteen-hour labour I had just been through. Tatti, by now, was asleep in a clear, plastic hospital cot by my bed. She looked so peaceful, her long eyelashes grazing her cheeks. Raw fear was surging through my veins. I had to get to Lucie. I pulled on my jeans and T-shirt and a nurse walked me through a labyrinth of corridors until, finally, I saw my daughter in a high-sided metal cot, screaming.

I can't remember much of what happened next, except for an overwhelming feeling that maybe I wasn't meant to have two children. Maybe the god I have never believed in was going to take Lucie away from me. My thinking was wrong. Part of me knew this, but the pain from giving birth, the withdrawal from the drugs and the overwhelming fear about Lucie coincided to make thinking rationally impossible.

We were later allowed to leave hospital. The incident was written off as unexplained and it wasn't until years later, when Toby had his first seizure, that I recognized what had happened in that room. A reflex anoxic seizure.

Off the Lorazepam, I lasted only a few more days, at home with Lucie and Tatti. I developed vertigo. The panic attacks increased. I could feel nothing but fear. I couldn't look after my girls. I couldn't look after myself. My sensory issues were magnified to a terrifying extent. Even the slightest noise, a cupboard door closing, a distant car, felt like an explosion. I was jumpy and nauseous. My heartbeat was so irregular, I was sure I was about to go into cardiac arrest.

Michael found me a doctor. He came to our flat and immediately admitted me to the Charter Nightingale Hospital to undergo a benzodiazepine withdrawal programme. Those little blue pills had rendered me unrecognizable, even to myself.

Lorazepam, the doctor told me, is habit forming. It is easy to become addicted. It shouldn't be used long-term. Withdrawal is harsh and should be done slowly, tapering the dose. It can be dangerous to stop cold turkey. I learn more about the drugs that had sent my life spinning out of control in this one conversation than I knew the whole time I was taking them.

I was twenty-three. The mother of two small girls – alone, confused and terrified. When I look at my own children – two of whom are now older than I was then – I realize I was no more than a child, but I had let everyone down . . .

Rehab – Spring 1993

I'm lying in a narrow, metal, single bed. The noises from the corridor scare me. They are hard to identify. I think I can hear someone crying. I know I can hear someone shouting. There's laughter too. I hate this scary alien place. I want to be at home. That's not true. I want not to be. I want to stop feeling and thinking and being. I don't want to be dead. Definitely not dead. I am not a risk to myself. I know this because when I went through the questionnaire with the nurse, she ticked a box saying I was not a risk to myself or others.

I can hear music. It's after 11 p.m. I'm surprised music is allowed. I'm never going to get to sleep. Literally never. The door opens a bit and a nurse holding a torch pops her head round the door. Seriously? They say I need rest, that I am exhausted, and then they come to shine torches into my eyes. I'm never going to get to sleep. Literally never.

I see midnight and 1 a.m. and 2 a.m. Then I am hovering on the edge of asleep and awake. The bed crinkles under me.

I know I am not dreaming, but also I know I am not thinking lucidly. It's at this point in between where magic can happen. Here I feel calm, safe and warm. Here I am not irritated by the roughness of the sheets or the way my pyjama top is riding up under the covers. Here I just am. It feels peaceful. Calm. It feels OK. Maybe it will all be OK.

Another torch in my face! It feels like a slap. I sit up, quickly.

'Go back to sleep,' a second nurse says. 'I was just checking you're OK.'

'I am not OK,' I snap.

'Get some sleep. Things will seem better in the morning.'

I am never going to get to sleep. Literally never.

I get up to go to the bathroom. It's opposite my bed. It's a small room with a bath, a basin and a loo. There's a shower over the bath and a glass panel to stop water from the shower splashing onto the floor. It makes getting in and out of the bath difficult. I splash cold water on my face. I am on the edge of a panic attack. I feel the telltale signs. A warm, slightly tickly feeling spreads through my chest. It feels quite pleasant when it begins, but then I recognize it for what it is and terror grips me.

Maybe I'm dying. Standing in front of the mirror, my heart is racing. Maybe I'll have a heart attack and they'll find me in the morning. The doctors swear there's nothing wrong with my heart. I don't believe them. I am sure they are wrong.

I walk back to my bed, holding my hand against my face so I won't accidentally catch a glimpse of the darkness behind the window.

Yesterday a nurse told me that there are lots of people here who are terrified of looking into windows in the dark. Apparently it's because they have taken a bad batch of Ecstasy that has sent them a bit mad. Drug-induced psychosis. That's its proper name. I wonder if I have this too. I feel as if I am a minute away from madness.

The drugs I took weren't bought in a dark club from a

dealer. They were given to me by a Harley Street doctor. I didn't ask what they were. Why would I? He told me the little blue pills would make me better and I believed him. They haven't made me better. They've put me in this frightening place.

At 6 a.m. a nurse comes in. She is holding a tiny plastic cup with two yellow pills. She holds it out to me and pours me a cup of water from the jug by my bed.

'I'll take them in a minute,' I say, thinking I can wash them down the sink when she leaves.

'They're a controlled drug,' she tells me. 'I need to see you swallow them.'

I start to shake. 'I don't want to take them.'

'Why not? They'll make you better.'

I am on a withdrawal programme. Each week I will take a lower dose of these pills that have me in their grip until one day I won't need them anymore.

'I'm scared to,' I say.

'You can bring that up with your therapist later. Just take these ones and you can tell her how you feel this morning.'

I can't take them. I panic. I want to run but there's nowhere to run to.

The nurse is coaxing and cajoling. 'I'm going to have to stay here until you take them,' she sighs. 'And I've got a lot I should be getting on with.'

I tip the pills into my mouth and put them under my tongue. I take a gulp of water. The bitter taste of the pills is making me want to gag.

'Lift your tongue up,' the nurse says. I learn later they are wise to anything I might think of. Not wanting to be caught out, I take another mouthful of water and let the pills wash upwards in my mouth.

I open my mouth and show her the pills are gone. 'Well done,' she says. 'Now get dressed and you can go and get some breakfast.'

I lie in a hot bath, trying to quell the rising panic. I count to ten and then start again. I must be up to five hundred in tens, but the panic won't subside.

I need to eat but I don't want to go down to the restaurant. Yesterday I watched the girls with eating disorders in there. They sat at a table on their own with their counsellor. The other patients, the depressed ones, the anxious ones, the addicts like me, can sit anywhere we like. The ED girls have to sit where they are told. Their counsellor watches their every bite.

I don't eat a lot. I can't eat when I am feeling this out of control. My therapist asked me questions about food. She said I have 'issues' with it. I told her I didn't, I just liked the food I liked and didn't like the rest.

I pull on my jeans and a pink sweatshirt that has a picture of a teddy bear on it and swirly writing that reads *The American Dream*. I put on my pink Converse high-tops and push my hair back into a ponytail.

I walk to the kitchen down the corridor. It's like I imagine a communal kitchen in student halls to be. There's a microwave oven, a toaster and three kettles. People here make a lot of tea and coffee. There's a big table in the middle of the room with ten chairs around it and there's a large, battered brown sofa in the corner.

This room is always busy. People meet here before and after meals, before and after group therapy and before and during the long evening hours when nothing much is happening. Everyone carries books and folders. The books are all about improving oneself. They have titles like *Feel the Fear and Do it Anyway*.

I have brought my own books with me. *What Katy Did* and *Mallory Towers* are hidden in the chest of drawers beneath my clothes. I don't want the others to think I'm a baby, reading books like that, or that there's something wrong with my brain. I brought them because I find them comforting. I don't think anyone else will understand that. They are 'working the programme' and there's no time for self-indulgence.

I light a cigarette. Pretty much everyone smokes here or eats chocolate. I met a girl last night called Sara, who was a veteran of places like this. She was my age, but this was her third attempt.

'When I was in rehab in the States,' she says, her accent sort of mid-Atlantic, 'we weren't allowed to have caffeine, cigarettes or chocolate.'

She looks at me accusingly. I'm aware of the half-eaten bar of Dairy Milk and mug of coffee in front of me and the half-smoked cigarette in my hand.

'It's much purer there.' She expects a response.

'Why don't you go back then?' I want to say this, but I don't. Instead I just nod and look serious as if I am contemplating what this must have been like.

A male person comes in. I feel awkward calling him a man. I don't know why, but it's one of the words I don't like. He's not a boy. Not like my friends. He's older than us. Maybe thirty or so. Often I settle on 'guy' when trying to describe someone like this. Men are old – at least fifty. Boys stop being boys at around twenty-five and I don't know what to call the ones in the middle.

This guy is holding a can of Diet Coke and a copy of the *Telegraph*. He sits on the sofa and starts doing the cryptic crossword. I like the look of him. I want him to be my friend. He looks less scary than the others. His clothes aren't fashionable. He isn't a rehab veteran. He looks as awkward as I do. I smile at him and he smiles back.

'Fuck,' someone says. 'It's ten o'clock. We're going to be late.'

People shuffle out of the kitchen on their way to their various groups. I report to the nurses' station and tell them I'm ready for my next set of pills. This time it's sleeping pills. Part of my treatment is to sleep for twenty hours a day for the first two weeks. I am clinically exhausted, they say. I hate taking the sleeping pills as they don't always work and I am left tired and stressed, as I was last night.

A nurse walks me back to my room and I take the pills. When she leaves I put my pyjamas back on and get under the covers. I look at the copy of *The Road Less Travelled* someone has left by the bed. There's a sticky note on it. *Thought you might like this, luv Sara xx.* I open the book and begin to read, but soon the words are swimming on the page and my eyelids feel heavy.

I wake at 7 p.m. I'm thirsty. I climb back into my jeans and sweatshirt and, not bothering to put on any shoes, I go to the kitchen to make some tea. Thankfully it's empty, everyone must be having supper in the conservatory downstairs.

I miss my girls. I feel so guilty leaving them like this. They are so small. Tatti is only a month old. Lucie is just three. They are coming to visit at the weekend. I feel close to tears. I have let them down. My hand shakes as I pour water over the teabag and heap in three sugars. I need it to help me wake up. I grab a Bourbon biscuit from the open pack on the work-top and sit down at the table.

The guy from earlier comes in. He sits opposite me. He's still got the can of Diet Coke and the newspaper. I see the crossword is almost all filled in. He doesn't say anything. I hate silences like this.

'Hi,' I say. He doesn't look up from the paper.

'Hello.'

'I'm Laura,' I persist.

'Tim,' he replies.

'I'm just going to drink this, then I'm going downstairs to get some food,' I tell him. I am sure he isn't in the least bit interested.

'I fancy a Chinese,' he replies. My mind darts to chilli beef, sweet and sour chicken and egg fried rice. My tummy rumbles.

'They don't have that here,' I say.

'Yeah, I know. But I'm allowed out. So I'm going to get a takeaway.'

'Gosh, you're so lucky,' I say.

'I wouldn't say that,' he replies as he leaves the room.

CHAPTER FIVE

November 2015

I'm on my way to London. I follow my usual routine. I arrive at the Wells Deli, just as it opens at 8 a.m.

'We could set our watch by you,' says Jason from behind a counter filled with delicious-looking cakes and muffins.

I laugh, but inwardly feel trapped by the fact that he's right. I am a prisoner to my routines. Why can't I be like normal people and go to the coffee shop at different times? It has to be this way otherwise I cannot get on with the rest of my day. It would feel as wrong as going to a meeting in a bikini or eating supper first thing in the morning. The fact is, if I don't go to the coffee shop at 8 a.m., 11 a.m. and 4.50 p.m. my day is ruined. It is having a map for the day that makes me feel safe. But it's also a prison I have built for myself. Within its walls, I feel claustrophobic and sad. My habit is also expensive and I'm trying – and failing – to save money.

I love the coffee shop. Nothing changes. The blond wood floors are always clean. The tables, with their mismatched chairs, are always in the same place, never moved around like in some other restaurants. Every interaction is the same. As I arrive whoever is on the till will ask whether I'd like my usual and I will nod. Waiting for my coffee, I will sit on a high stool by the counter and look at my phone to answer emails and texts, and to see what's trending on Twitter. These interludes in my day regulate my anxiety. All is fine if I am where I am meant to be at the right time.

After my coffee has been made, tested, sent back for less froth and more milk, I go to catch my train. At the station, which, with its cafe, honesty library and colourful stationmaster, is like something from a 1960s children's storybook, I pick up a copy of the *Daily Telegraph*. I have a story in it today. It's my coming-out piece.

My train is not due to arrive for another ten minutes. I stand against a wall at the far side of the platform and nervously flick through the pages until I see it. A picture of me taken in the dining room at home takes up practically half the page. I slam it shut, in the way you quickly close a door when you see a spider scuttle across the floor.

I slowly open it again. My face is still there, looking back at me. I wander out into the car park. Suddenly I need more space around me. My phone is pinging, even more than is usual, but I'm juggling coffee, bags and the newspaper, so I try to ignore it.

The feeling stirred in me by seeing the article is a new one. It feels a little like scared, but different from the usual, almost omnipresent, fear. Maybe it's because coming out has left me exposed. Perhaps this is M's *vulnerable*.

Tim and I talked about feelings last night. He's begun to ask me more questions recently.

'What do you feel when you see a spider in the bath?' he asks.

'It activates the get-help protocol,' I reply.

He laughs.

'What do you feel if I surprise you with a new grey jumper? And God help me if it's not grey.'

'It makes me feel overwhelmed,' I say. Tim looks at me and says nothing. I think he wants more from my answer. 'I think it's because I haven't had time to accommodate the idea of this particular jumper in my life. It's different when I buy it myself because in the shop I will have considered how it will fit with my other grey jumpers.'

He hasn't yet asked any big questions about emotions, such as how I experience love. The truth is it frightens me. What if I don't love people properly? What if I'm missing out on the most essential part of life. Love is seen as the driving force of our world.

I wonder if I was alone in having real sympathy for the Prince of Wales when he uttered *whatever love means* in the famous interview he gave with the then Lady Diana Spencer on their engagement. Do I love Tim? I think so. I am used to him and his presence often helps me find my emotional neutral. I like to know he is there. He is certainly the only person whose presence I can tolerate for extended periods. I imagine telling him this. Telling him that I think I love him because he helps me achieve neutrality. Years ago he would have stormed out; now I think he'd just laugh.

How do we know what love is? As a child I was hugely frustrated by not knowing if everyone experienced colour in the same way I did. Just because we all call something blue, how do we know we see it in the same way? When I learned of colour blindness I was enchanted. It, along with spontaneous combustion, became one of my early special interests and I would ask everyone I met if they were colour blind. Isn't it the same with love? How do we know if we all feel it the same way?

The train arrives and I get on. I find my usual seat, halfway along a middle carriage, to the left by the window. I unpack my iPad, put my phone on the little pull-down tray table and place my coffee next to it. It's cold now, but I don't mind; it can take me three hours to finish a coffee and I like it at every temperature as long as the initial recipe is right.

I open the *Telegraph* again and flick through to my feature. The picture shows me in a crisp white shirt, one hand resting under my chin. My glasses are next to me on the dining room table I painted during a brief obsession with make-do-and-mend and I am looking over my open laptop. Behind me – perhaps significantly, perhaps accidentally – are two doors: one open, the other closed. The caption under the picture reads: *Laura James was diagnosed with autism as an adult, years after constantly feeling she was different from others.*

I can't quite believe I have written it. That I have bared my soul in a national newspaper. Logically, I know I did it for good reasons. As a journalist, I recognized it was a good story. When I tried to find other autistic women like me, I couldn't, so this was a way to reach out to others like me, to tell them they are not alone. I wanted to tell people in my life about my diagnosis and couldn't find it in myself to do it over and again. This was a way of doing it in one hit.

Looking at the newspaper now, it feels like the worst idea I have ever had. I feel exposed, as if everyone on the train knows my innermost thoughts. There's a man in the aisle opposite reading the *Telegraph*. Eventually he will find his way onto my pages. Will he read them with interest or will he flick past, writing it off as a woman's piece? Which is better? I don't know.

I'm ignoring the bleeping of my phone, something I usually find impossible. It is part of me. A symbiotic, love/hate relationship. An addiction. I am at once brilliant and terrible at answering messages. If I am engaged with someone I will answer immediately, so quickly they can't keep up. If I am unsure, I will take days, sometimes weeks, to return a message. When I am in that confusing stage of trying to work out if I want to build a friendship with someone, I can take months to answer. This alone is one reason I struggle to maintain friendships.

The train trundles through Cambridgeshire, then Hertfordshire and eventually makes its way into London, whizzing past Finsbury Park until it slows down at the Emirates stadium, home to Arsenal. I am always puzzled by sport, football in particular. How can it ignite such passion? I lack the competitive gene. Maybe it's because I was so clumsy at school and was always picked last for a team. Maybe it's because I have never felt a team spirit, have never been linked to anyone in the primal way sport seems to join people. Who knows? The idea of supporting a team is alien to me. How can you feel part of something that has nothing to do with you?

The train stops in the tunnel on the approach to King's Cross. I hate it when this happens. I feel my heart rate rise and sweat prickle on the back of my neck. My breathing becomes faster. I look out of the window to assess the gap between the side of the train and the tunnel wall. Another train is stationary next to us. There seems to be no gap, no way out. My claustrophobia overwhelms me. I am gripped with fear. I cup my hands over my mouth and breathe in deeply. What would happen if we became stuck like this? How would they get us out? Would they walk us to the front of the train? But this train coupled to another at Cambridge. I am in the back section. No one has ever been stuck on a train forever – right? My breathing is too fast. I try to slow it, but can't. My heart is beating irregularly. I feel too hot. I tear off my coat. I put my head between my knees. I think I might faint. I'm aware I am drawing attention to myself, a feeling I hate, but I just can't stop. I get up and walk up and down the aisle, trying to calm myself.

Just when I can take it no longer the train groans and begins to move. I try to slow my breathing. We pull into the station and I stay in my seat to avoid the rush to the door. Once out into the fresh air, I take a deep breath in and feel my mind slow down. I stand in the taxi queue, hoping I won't get one of the new claustrophobic Mercedes taxis. When this happens I let the person behind me go in front. I simply would not cope with being trapped in a metal box where the windows don't open and someone else is in charge of whether I can leave or not.

I get a good cab and within fifteen minutes or so am walking through the door of the private members' club I use as a base when I'm in London. It's a solution Tim and I agreed was right; it is cheaper, easier and a whole lot nicer than renting an office.

I immediately feel at home. The staff know me well. It's never too hot, too cold or too noisy. The menu rarely changes, the tea is good and they know how to make my coffee. I have an hour to go until my meeting. I like to be early whenever I can as it gives me the opportunity to transition in peace. The journey from Norfolk to London takes around three and a half hours door-to-door and I am on my guard the entire time. Waiting for a delay, a stopped train, a lack of cabs, a traffic jam.

Sitting in my favourite seat, upstairs in a quiet corner, drinking a cup of tea and trying to decide if I can face a chocolate biscuit, I look at my phone. The home screen is full of messages. My eyes graze them. There are smiley faces, kisses, WOWs and lots of messages of congratulation, literally hundreds of them. Some of the names I recognize, many I don't.

Autistic women – or those who suspect they might be on the spectrum – have messaged me on Twitter, on Facebook and via email. My phone rings and I jump. It's a producer from BBC Scotland. He asks if I'll talk about my autism on the next day's breakfast show. I tell him I have no Scottish links, but he says it doesn't matter – they'll get someone from a Scottish charity on too. The next call is from BBC Hereford and Worcester. I'm not even sure I could actually pinpoint Worcester on a map, but still they feel my *Telegraph* piece is interesting. I feel pleased that my instinct was right: it was a story that needed to be told; autistic women cannot continue to be invisible. We need to be seen and heard.

I stare at my phone, reading the things people have written.

We have always known there was something different about our daughter, who is now 13. My wife and I have taken her to many doctors, but have been made to feel as if we are making it up or are overbearing parents. Reading your article in the Telegraph *today was like looking at my daughter. I sent a link to my wife who agrees and we are now going to make an appointment with our GP. Thank you for bringing these issues to our attention.*

As you probably know, I have a son with Asperger's. Last time I saw you, at Sarah's birthday, it occurred to me you behave in a very Aspie way. As your life seems so good and you always appear happy, I didn't feel it was right I should say anything. Now, though, I just wanted to say I'm pleased you have the answers you've been looking for. Perhaps next time I spot someone on the spectrum, I'll try to raise it in conversation.

I receive an email from a freelance journalist I know. It says: *In just one little article you will have given such relief – and such hope – to so many women. Sometimes makes the job feel so worthwhile doesn't it?*

A designer I work with emails: *Fascinated to read your* Telegraph *piece. Lovely to hear you feel you know yourself a bit better now.*

M messages me: *Congratulations, Laura – the article looks great!*

The daughter of a friend who has been struggling with depression and has recently been diagnosed with ADHD emails. It says: *My mum sent me the link to your article. Great to see someone being so honest and brave to talk about themselves as you do! So well written too! Congratulations!!*

No one says anything negative. I start to breathe a bit more slowly. This might be OK after all.

I have come out and I am relieved. When anyone asks about my diagnosis, or my story, I will be able to send a link to the piece, and there is an elegance to this as a solution that I really like.

My meetings pass in a blur. Until the last. It's with Louisa, the press officer for the National Autistic Society. I like her immediately. I am so grateful to have someone so plugged into the autism world all to myself for a couple of hours. She was a huge help with background information for my piece and tells me she's received a number of calls about it. I start to feel a little more comfortable with what I have done. The messages show that I have touched a nerve, that people are finding it helpful, that autism in women and girls is a subject that needs and deserves more attention.

I'm exhausted when I arrive back at King's Cross. I begin

to feel a telltale prickliness inside. It begins in my chest and radiates through my arms. My senses are heightened. The sound of a man coughing is rebounding around my head. The scrape of suitcase wheels on the shiny station floor. The station announcements. The lights are too bright, the sounds too loud. The smell of fast food is cloying. I feel like I can't escape.

This is a safety announcement. It is not permitted to cycle, skateboard or rollerblade within the station building.

I go to the loo to try to rebalance. The hand driers are screaming their tuneless song. There's a queue. I am assaulted by the cheap perfume of the woman in front of me. Its synthetic notes are stuck in my nose and I feel as if the smell will linger forever. I race back down the escalator and into the cool evening air.

I am going to miss my train, but I don't care. Nothing could get me to go back into the station right now. It is just after five-thirty and I know the train will be crowded, so I reason with myself that I should wait for the next one. I feel guilty, though. It means I will be home later and that Tim and the boys will again have to have supper without me.

I hate uncertainty of any kind. I like to know exactly what is going on in my world and what will happen next. Because of this I feel the need to inform Tim of each stage of my day. Almost hourly updates by phone or by text message. I'm sure he just thinks, *she's out for the day, she'll be back late*, and that's it. I for some reason, however, am compelled to ring him between meetings, to tell him exactly what is happening in my day and to hear what is happening in his. Nothing drives me more crazy than learning something when I get home that I could have been told hours before.

Communication is an ongoing battle between us. I need to talk, he does not. I guess it's the classic Mars versus Venus thing, with an added dash of autistic versus neurotypical thrown in for good measure. Typically, I'll ring him four times during the day. Once to say my train has arrived and I am in London. Once to tell him about my first meeting, then again after my second. I'll ring another time to tell him which train I intend to get home and then either once I am on the train or when I reach Downham Market and I'm getting into the car. Between these calls I will often message him.

Often I pepper the call with excuses. I'll ask what he wants to do about supper or give him some nugget of information about the meeting I have just attended. I know it is torture for him to have these mindless conversations, but it is equally painful for me not to. I imagine there is information he is keeping from me. The fact that Tim also has the world's worst telephone manner – an awkwardness and brusqueness that leads me to believe a huge disaster has happened and my family is in real jeopardy – does not help matters.

I can't bring myself to tell him that the idea of getting on the train is too much, so instead I wait a few minutes, until after it's left, and ring and say I've only just got to the station.

I sit on a wall outside the station and light a cigarette. I'm still on the tipping point of a meltdown. A woman approaches me and asks if I have any spare change. She is thin, her face etched with lines she is too young to have collected. There is no life in her eyes. She stares at me without hope, expecting rejection at best, abuse at worst.

I look at her and feel utterly overwhelmed by the world. I get this feeling sometimes. It is fleeting and usually lasts no more than an hour. The best phrase I have found to describe it is *humanity depression*. It descends when I see just exactly what we are capable of doing to each other. It creeps into my chest when I see abusive posts on Twitter. And when I hear the news about refugees living in dirty tented villages filled with fear and danger, with countries refusing to take them in. Refusing to offer them sanctuary in a land of plenty where we have houses for our cars. What does that do to a human being?

There's much talk about autism and empathy. One school of thought is that autistic people do not feel it. I am easily confused by abstract concepts such as empathy. I cannot put myself in someone else's shoes, but I am probably one of the most compassionate people you are likely to meet. My compassion, though, comes in the form of practical support. I don't have the tools to say 'there, there' and listen endlessly to a problem being hashed and rehashed.

Tony Attwood is in no doubt that those with Asperger's feel empathy. For him the issue is that often they may feel it too acutely. He told me: 'Oh yes, absolutely autistic people feel empathy. Too much. More than neurotypicals. I think some of the social withdrawal [typical of those with Asperger's] may be because of an acute sensitivity to negative emotions in others. It's the equivalent of an emotional cold for the person with Asperger's; it's contagious. They are infected and they get the flu. It's as if people with Asperger's have a sixth sense for despair, anguish, irritation, negativity in other people. They can amplify these feelings and take them on board and realize it's because they've been with so and so.

'Solitude can be a way of cutting this down. So the impulse towards solitude isn't purely because of social confusion and social performance.'

My humanity depression is, I believe, a form of empathy. It is an inability to cope with the pain of others. It overwhelms me, makes me feel unsure of the world and unsure of my place within it. The unusual way I experience empathy leaves me confused about human relationships. I find it painful when I cannot second-guess how someone else is feeling or what they are thinking. Humans give out conflicting messages and this blows my autistic brain.

When someone who is clearly angry or upset insists, through gritted teeth, that they are *fine*, I don't know what to do or say. I know they are not fine.

I open my purse and give the homeless woman some change. She smiles at me with real warmth. An older woman, close by, turns to me.

'She'll only spend it on drugs, you know,' she says. 'You shouldn't give money to people like that.'

I hate being told things like this. I hate people interfering and, in the midst of a sensory overload, this woman, with her loud patterned sweater and even louder voice, is grating on my nerves, pushing me one step closer towards meltdown.

'I'm talking to you,' she says slightly aggressively, as I continue to ignore her. 'It's rude not to answer.'

I just need to be in the quiet and in the dark and I am hours from home. I get up and walk away. Away from her bigotry and hatred. Away from the station, from my train. And away from home. I find a quiet coffee shop on a side street and order a bottle of water.

When I was a child, my meltdowns were explosions. I would kick and scream, throw myself to the floor, cry so hard I couldn't catch my breath. They were loud, violent and messy. Now when I have a meltdown it's an implosion. I feel all the same emotions: the need to escape; being unable to control my feelings, my environment and myself, but there's nothing spectacular to see when I'm having a meltdown. I may leave the room slightly more quickly than I would ordinarily, but despite being a huge deal to me, there really is very little for anyone else to witness.

Looking for Marina – Summer 1995

I stand on the doorstep and hesitate before I ring the bell. I've waited all my life for this moment and now I'm wondering if I've made a huge mistake. Maybe some things are better left alone. Perhaps nothing will ever be as good as the fantasy.

'All right?' Tim asks, putting his hand on my arm.

'I'm not sure I want to do this,' I say, my voice trembling. 'Shall we go and get a drink so I can think about it?'

'If that's what you really want, but you've come this far.'

It is what I want. I don't like it when people try to talk me out of a decision I've made. I'm generally sure of what I want and what I don't want and right now I don't want this. I'm twenty-five. I think I should be able to make my own decisions.

We walk through the streets of Notting Hill. I walk quickly, wanting to put as much distance between me and the house Marina lives in as I can. What if I don't like what I find there?

I have often wondered what my childhood would have been like if Marina had kept me with her. Would simply being with the woman who had given birth to me have given me a sense of belonging? I think it would have. I imagine if you know where you have come from, you have a better idea of where you are going. You may not like your family. You may not get on with them, but you would belong to them. They would be yours and you would be theirs.

From the snippets I have learned about Marina, from what my parents have told me, and the file I was given by Social Services, I imagine my life would have been less structured. I think it would have been more creative. Freer. Maybe I'm wrong. Perhaps all adopted children build an alternative story in their heads. One that suits their view of what their other life would have been like. Should have been like.

I heard a documentary once on Radio 4. A little girl was being interviewed. She must have been around five or six. 'My other mummy is a princess,' the girl said proudly, 'and she lives in a castle.' There was a certainty to her voice and I experienced an understanding that was new to me. While I am too old to believe in fairy princesses, part of me will always, I think, hold on to the fact Marina was someone special, somehow perfect.

Tim and I find a corner table in a small cafe. He orders a Diet Coke. I order tea. We are quiet for a while then he asks: 'Have you changed your mind?'

'I'm not sure,' I say, annoyed that my tea is too weak and the sugar is lumps rather than sachets. 'I'm just a bit worried about what happens once I let her into my life. What if I don't like her? What if she's a complete nightmare? I have convinced myself things will be better if I have some context, but what if that context is the chaos of a selfish, shambolic woman?'

'Do you think you might actually be worried about it being the other way round?' he asks. 'I mean, do you think you might be worried that actually she might not want you?'

The thought hadn't occurred to me. 'Not really,' I say, pushing the disappointing tea to one side. 'But she might have got married again, I suppose, and her husband might not know about me, so I guess that's a possibility.'

'Would that feel like a bigger rejection?' Tim asks. He is nervous of saying the wrong thing and is toying with the edge of the gingham tablecloth. 'I mean, that she was not what used to be called a gymslip mother.'

'I don't think I feel rejected at all,' I say truthfully.

He looks back at me uncomprehending. Tim's adoption has stalked him throughout his life and was something most therapists he had seen over the years had deemed central to the depression he had been hospitalized for.

He didn't see it that way. Or so he said. But the picture he created was confusing. At any one time his adoption could be an utter irrelevance or fundamental to his own sense of alienation. One day he would dismiss its importance as, at best, tangential. The next he would lament the absence of any emotional context. He would dismiss never having known his biological father as unimportant. The next day, his mood blacker, he would write a song about the US airman who left his mother alone and pregnant, with no regard for the life inside and the man he would become.

I find this all rather strange and confusing. My feelings about Marina are rooted in logic. Giving up a baby for adoption doesn't feel like a rejection to me. How can you reject a person you don't really know? It's not about the child. It's about the circumstances.

Tim cannot understand this approach. He finds it strange my reactions are so muted. We've been living together for around six months and I'm finding it so hard. Everything he does is governed by feelings rather than logic. He is constantly chasing the good feelings, the next adventure. He lives by the catchphrase 'more, now, again'. Nothing is ever enough.

I feel I constantly disappoint him. I am not adventurous enough. I don't live fast enough. His temper is quick and fiery. His anger scares me. I don't understand how he lives with that fire inside him.

I think he finds me childish. I feel homesick, but I don't know what for. I think I've made a mistake. A big one. I don't want to go back to my ex-husband, but I don't want to stay here.

I have caused so much turmoil for my girls, who are now forced to divide their time between their two parents. Was it worth it? I don't think so. I am awash with fear all the time. I walk on eggshells. I wonder what Tim's mood will be like today. Will he bathe me in sunlight and the glow of his love or will he be angry, snarling, quick to criticize?

I'm slightly afraid he will be cross with me now. He doesn't look cross though. Today he seems to be kind Tim, playing the role of supportive boyfriend as we seek out my past. I think he sees life as a series of scenes in a film. The setting for today's scene will be the fondant-coloured houses of Elgin Crescent. The backdrop will be a perfect blue sky, the summer sunshine warming our backs as we walk. The stars will be Marina and me, with him nominated for an award as best supporting actor.

He is looking out of the window. He has a photographer's eye. He drinks in everything he sees. I think sight is his most important sense. It's as if he wants to see all the things. Always.

When he is driving along the motorway through the Chilterns on the way to see his parents, he is on the lookout for the red kites that have recently started breeding there. When we're in a restaurant he will stare at the waitress with the good legs, but also notice small details I try hard not to see. As a child I would see everything. If I looked at a lawn it was as if I could see every blade of grass. It was too much. Too overwhelming. I learned to blur my eyes, so everything became softer. So I didn't have to process so much information. Now I always carry a book with me so I can read, or I find some small detail – in this case in the Coke can – to look at.

When we're sitting at home on the sofa he will look at me as if I am a rare and precious thing. Such scrutiny makes me feel uncomfortable. I have always had a problem making eye contact. My childhood was punctuated by grown-ups saying, 'Look at me when I'm talking to you.' Locking eyes with Tim is almost painful. It is as if he wants to drink in my soul. There's a hunger in him that scares me.

Leaving my husband for him has caused so much anger. Everyone is shouting at me. My parents, his parents, our friends. Everyone is furious. My husband has filed for divorce. I'm terrified. Everything is so legal and I feel like I'm in big trouble. How is my life spiralling so far out of control?

Starting an affair with Tim is the most reckless thing I have ever done. I can't even explain quite how it happened. It's clichéd, but I guess I really was hit by a coup de foudre and swept off my feet. I can see why they call it falling in love, because it really did feel like falling. I fell for his intelligence. I had never met anyone who knew so much. But the thing about falling is eventually you have to land and it's not always somewhere soft.

I don't think I will stay with Tim forever. Life is too chaotic. I can't cope with the ups and downs his moods bring. I need stability. As in the Rupert Brooke poem, 'The Old Vicarage, Grantchester', I need certainty and quiet kind. He needs adventure and we will always be in a push-me-pull-me cycle of not being able to give what the other needs.

'What do you want to do?' he asks eventually, impatiently. 'Go home, go and see a film? Go back and knock on the door?'

Mostly I want to do nothing, to make no decisions, to just sit here. I also want to make Tim happy. At the Charter Nightingale Hospital my therapist said I was a 'people pleaser', that

I was so frightened of disappointing others that I went along with things that are bad for me.

Tim is restless. There's a muscle going in his cheek and he is bouncing his knee up and down as if he wants to run, wants something to happen.

'Let's go and knock on the door,' I say. His smile is warm. It was the right answer. He is happy.

The door has both a bell and a knocker. I don't know which to choose. I find it so confusing when people have both. The house facade is pale yellow, like the lemon French Fancies. I like pink ones best – houses and cakes – but lemon would be my second choice. I go for the bell. The knocker might be there for decorative purposes, but the bell is too unattractive for that. I hear it ring: a long, sharp ring. We wait. Nothing happens. No yapping dog. No footsteps. Nothing.

Emboldened by the lack of response I use the knocker instead. Again we wait.

'Of course there's no reason to think she still lives here,' I say. The only reason we are here is because it's the address on my birth certificate, but that was twenty-five years ago. She has probably moved on.

'We could knock next door and ask if they know her,' Tim says. As a journalist (something I have longed to be) he thinks nothing of pitching up at a complete stranger's house and asking questions. I feel nervous at the idea.

'Why would we say we are asking?'

'Don't worry, I'll think of something.' He is already making his way down the steps.

The neighbouring house is white with a glossy black front door. It is well kept, just like the woman who answers it. She is in her early sixties and wearing a cream silk blouse and a tweed skirt. Her shoes are sensible but look expensive. Her greying hair is perfectly in place. She looks at us with curiosity.

'Yes?' she says, slightly raising one eyebrow.

'Hi,' Tim says. His voice is steady and assured. 'We're looking to trace someone who lived next door in the early 1970s and wondered if you happened to have been here then. If you might have known her. Her name's Marina.'

'She's dead,' the woman replies.

I feel faint. Of all the possible outcomes, how could I not have considered this one? I thought she would either be here still or would have moved away and I would either spend ages tracking down her new address or the trail would go cold and she would be lost to me forever. But dead? That really wasn't a possibility I'd considered. Why would I have done? No one should be dead so young.

The woman's expression softens. 'Are you OK?'

'Yes,' I say. 'I'm fine. Just a little shocked.' She seems re-assured. I don't know if it's my accent, which becomes even plummier when I'm nervous, or curiosity on her part but she invites us in.

We stand in the hallway. The floor is tiled in black and white marble. 'Would you like some tea?' she asks. I say I would. 'I'll put lots of sugar in. It's good when you've had a shock.'

Tim says no to tea. He doesn't drink it or coffee. He only drinks Diet Coke. Gallons of it. He used to drink a lot of Jack Daniel's too, but as I can't have alcohol while I'm on my withdrawal programme, he doesn't drink so much anymore.

The woman tells us her name is Gertrude. She has lived in the house for years. She knew Marina well.

'She led a rackety life.' Gertrude's accent is Hungarian I think. I look around the room, which is perfectly ordered. I feel comfortable here. Comfortable enough to tell her the truth.

'Marina was my mother.' Gertrude looks surprised. I can see her grasping for the right words. They're not coming easily.

'I was adopted,' I say, rather pointlessly.

'Marina was difficult,' Gertrude says. 'Her little boy was lovely though. He spent a lot of time here.'

This is new information. I need to process it. Marina had a son that she kept. I knew she had five boys, but I thought she had left them in America.

'What happened to him?' I ask. I'm wondering if he died with her. This seems unlikely, but my brain doesn't feel like it's working too well.

'He lives in Clarendon Cross and teaches t'ai chi in Holland Park,' she says, handing me tea in a pretty china cup. 'You'll catch him there this afternoon if you'd like to meet him. Go to the cafe and ask for Conn. Everyone there knows him.'

While I drink my tea, Gertrude's voice washes over me as she talks to Tim about how the area has changed over the years. About her own children and her husband, a jazz musician. I can't speak. I have slipped into my safe space, where words elude me.

'We'll take a walk over to the park then,' Tim says, thanking Gertrude for the tea and her time.

Outside, the air feels warm after the cool drawing room.

'I can't believe it,' I say to Tim. 'Dead.'

'Yes. I'm sorry,' he says. He moves to hug me but thinks better of it.

I'm not sure how I feel. I say nothing. We thread our way through Notting Hill, back to the car as the sun starts to dip below the rooftops. When Tim turns the key in the ignition the radio comes on. It's playing 'Life on Mars'.

Tim pulls out of the parking space and I gaze out of the window. That's that, I think. We pull up outside the entrance to Holland Park. I used to bring Lucie here to the One O'clock Club when she was just a year old.

'Want to go and find your brother?' Tim asks. I nod and we get out.

CHAPTER SIX

March 2016

Three phones are ringing and I can't decide which one to pick up first. Fridays are usually quiet. A magazine I work on is going to bed on Monday and there's confusion over which cover picture we will use. I have a piece I need to write on etiquette for another magazine and have agreed to make a video on what it feels like to become overwhelmed by sensory stimuli for the *Guardian* online and the National Autistic Society. I need to write an outline about an incident in a restaurant where I became overwhelmed.

There is too much to do and I can't figure out the order to do it in. Tim and I answer a phone each and I let the call on my mobile go to voicemail. Both calls are quick and easy to deal with. They both relate to one of our PR clients. Someone wants a quick price check, the other an image.

It is quiet again. I tell Tim I'm feeling engulfed and don't know what to do next.

'Send me an email with a list of all the things you need to do and go and get a coffee. When you get back I'll have prioritized them for you.'

As I sit in the steamy fug of the coffee shop I begin to slow down. I feel less panicky. I know Tim will come up with a solution and, if I do exactly what he says, everything will get done. Tim is able to prioritize things in a way I find impossible. It is a skill he has that I don't.

When I get back home, there is a clear list on what to do and in what order.

I need to ring Lucy, Mary Berry's assistant, and arrange a time for a photo shoot. I need to book Eurostar tickets for another shoot we're doing in France in a couple of weeks with a French news journalist. I have to read a set of recipe proofs, send out a press release, write a piece on trends in colour and find a celebrity to interview for a piece on best-ever meals.

Many couples would struggle with being together all day, every day. We don't. We work easily together. We don't sugar-coat our criticisms. I can see when we are with others that they find this disconcerting, but I like how straightforward it is. We are always completely honest about how we feel the other is doing on a particular project. We are never unkind, but there is no mincing of words.

When I tell people about my autism or they read something I have written, one of the first points they raise is how unusual it is for someone with a condition characterized by communication difficulties to communicate for a living. I've thought a lot about this. It was one of the things that made me think twice about asking for an assessment. I love my job. I love the variety, the filling of empty pages, the decisions I have to take, the fascinating people I get to interview.

The key to why I find it easy is that there is a structure to everything. A feature needs to be a set number of words. An interview is not like a social conversation. I get to ask any question that pops into my head and it isn't seen as impolite. There is no hedging around a subject and little small talk.

Steve Silberman, author of the hugely successful *Neurotribes: The Legacy of Autism and How to Think Smarter About People Who Think Differently*, believes that a major workplace obstacle for those with autism is lack of support. He told me: 'Autistic people often face considerable challenges in the workplace. They need more pervasive accommodations, more comprehensive forms of support.

'I do think autism is a disability but I'm not saying autistic people aren't able. In terms of the social model of disability, if there are no wheelchair accessible bathrooms, then being in a wheelchair is really disabling, and if there are no accommodations made in education and the workplace, then being autistic is actually very disabling. I think that's the difference.'

My psychiatrist, Somayya Kajee, agrees. She told me: 'Generally, as with most people, autistic people have a lot to offer but it is about finding the right environment. I think sensory difficulties can be a problem. I've seen about five people in the last three months whose main reason for wanting the diagnosis was to aid employment.

'Some of them would fall at the first hurdle. They couldn't get through the interview process because they struggled socially or they were so anxious. But if they had managed to get through that part, then actually within the work environment they would also struggle because maybe things weren't how they wanted them to be or they got fixated in doing things in a particular way and they couldn't then adjust to doing them differently. They may have found it too noisy or that people made fun of them because they were different.

'So, without a doubt, I think if people have a diagnosis of autism and they can be placed in supported work or in a workplace where there is a level of understanding they can do well.

'It's the simple things. I remember with one woman we just suggested earphones, earplugs or headphones and having her desk slightly moved, into a corner. One man got to work and his parking space wasn't available and that sent him into a complete tailspin. So simple things like that go a long way. Interestingly, a lot of people with autism will find employment in a niche that they are really very good at, valuable and productive.'

Autism brings with it many problems, but it also brings many benefits. My ability to zone into one subject and pull out the salient facts quickly and easily is surely something all journalists need. My ability to spot a trend or see a pattern is a necessary skill for every aspect of the work I do.

My meticulous need for accuracy – and for all facts to be verifiable – is an important trait for someone who essentially disseminates information.

Somayya Kajee believes it is important to remember these benefits, these positives. She told me: 'I do think people with autism are just literally wired differently and not in a negative way. There isn't necessarily anything wrong. If we are looking at people with autism, they can struggle with a lot of things that are part of society's constructs – how things should be because the vast majority would agree that's how they should be.

'So it doesn't mean that you're wrong. Nobody wants to feel that they're different and no one wants to struggle with sensory things and with being so rigid. But there are a lot of people, for example, who use their ability to hyperfocus positively. And there are companies that positively discriminate.

'I think if you look at prognostic factors, people who find their niche and are able to put their energy into something they love, something that's meaningful, then they do get a lot out of it. It doesn't matter that they may not be as socially active, because they're getting joy and happiness from what they're doing. I guess it's about identifying those things and supporting people to do just that.'

I love my work, but does it bring me joy? I think a lot about the point of the future. I might not strive for huge personal happiness, but is it wrong that I don't try, even if it is just for Tim?

Sarah Wild believes autistic happiness is different. She says: 'We neurotypical people have to stop projecting what our concepts of happiness are onto the autistic population because autistic happiness is not the same.

'Neurotypical professionals have ideas about living independently, having a job, being economically viable, having friends. But they're all neurotypical indexes of happiness and no one has bothered to ask autistic people what makes them happy, what are the things they need to be able to function. That's the next thing that needs to come. Much more voice from the autistic community.'

I love interviewing people. I don't feel any different talking to a scientist than I do to a celebrity. It is a huge privilege to be able to ask questions of someone, whether those questions relate to genetics or the latest film they are starring in. Meeting experts is pure heaven for someone autistic. The access I am given to someone's knowledge never fails to make me happy. Even more so if they happen to know something about one of my current intense interests.

I have access and I have a voice. Something I try to use for good whenever I can. Of course I suffer from impostor syndrome. I am a girl with no O-levels, who can't add up and doesn't know exactly what a split infinitive is. I should not be allowed to do the things I do.

It would be a lie to say that I find everything at work easy. I don't. I struggle with things on a daily basis. My desk is in permanent chaos. I write things on pieces of paper and then spend hours upending bins trying to find those few scribbled words that seem meaningless to anyone else, but are essential for something I need to do.

I live in fear of some, but not all, deadlines. Sometimes the terror is so great that I don't hand something in on time purely because I am so stressed there is an end date in sight. It's not that I couldn't have met the deadline. Rather, it's that my anxiety at giving up control, of handing something in, will take over and I will become paralysed, taken over by autistic inertia, unable to finish my task and unable to start anything else. I stay stuck. It's only when someone – occasionally Tim, but often someone outside – makes me face up to the fact I need to take action quickly that I do.

I like things to go smoothly, because the vast majority of my socializing is done within my work setting, often on the phone. It matters hugely to me that no one is upset, so often I will find myself agreeing to take on unpaid work or go outside the remit of a contract simply to ensure no feathers are ruffled.

I have always felt unworthy and as if, at any minute, I will be found out. I've learned, however, that many neurotypical women feel this way too; it's not just an issue for autistic women, although we seem to feel it particularly keenly. In part, for me at least, it is anchored in my feeling of not being a grown-up, a proper person. But as I need to pay the bills I have learned to keep pretending.

All in all, though, the positives of my work life outweigh the negatives. I am always so grateful I don't have to suffer as I did when I worked in offices. That I have the freedom for most of the day to be myself.

Slowly I have begun to be honest about my autism with the people I work with. I've told my clients and will often tell someone I am interviewing if it feels relevant. I've learned that, by being honest, others feel more able to open up about their own issues or differences.

CHAPTER SEVEN

April 2016

I am exhausted. It feels relentless. My body is broken. My brain is broken. I have had enough. I don't want to die. I just want it all to stop. I want to stop being. I want to have not been born. I want to not be me. I want to be someone else. I try to remember what M has said about trying to stay in the moment and not spin out about what might happen. Her words on allowing myself to feel vulnerable whirl around my head.

'I want to go home,' I say out loud, to the empty room. I press the buzzer by my bed. The wait seems interminable. I twirl my hair around my finger. I haven't eaten for more than twenty-four hours and am desperate for some water.

'All OK?' a cheery healthcare assistant asks, as she pops her head round the door to my room.

'Am I allowed a drink?' My voice is croaky from not having spoken for a while. I can go for hours without speaking in a hospital setting. I partially shut down and become selectively mute.

'Best not,' she says, keen to be doing something else. 'They're going to come and take you down to theatre soon.'

'When is soon? Do you mean ten minutes or an hour?'

'Well, that depends.' She retreats a little further out of the door. Tim considers interjecting in some way but doesn't.

'What does it depend on? I need you to be exact. I can't cope with uncertainty.'

'I'll go and see,' she says. I see her eyes harden as she writes me off as trouble.

I know this means I won't see her again and I feel the hospital walls shrink in on me a little.

I look for a distraction and try to listen to an audiobook on my iPad. I wish I had my headphones, but because I came straight here from seeing my consultant I don't have all the things I need to keep me calm. I want Tim to go home and get them, but he's insisting on staying until I go down to theatre. I would rather have my headphones, scarf, pyjamas and books than him, but it feels unkind to say so. In situations like this, he often takes on the role of my unofficial translator. He anticipates what I need and tries to negotiate it for me.

When we first arrived we were shepherded into a waiting room. The local radio station was pumping out a mix of cheery chat and nondescript music. Every chair was filled with patients and friends or family. A dozen conversations were competing for attention in my ears and in my head. I couldn't screen them out. I hovered on the edge of an implosion.

'We must ring your mum,' an older woman was saying to a man holding a piece of bloodied gauze to his head.

'It can't be much longer,' a man said to a woman in a wheelchair who was wearing a floral nightdress that exposed legs riddled with varicose veins. I found them strangely fascinating and had to try hard not to stare.

Bleeps and buzzers were sounding. Noises were merging. I hear each individual sound, all the time, wherever I am and, like a too-tight shoe that rubs, the pain grows the longer I am exposed to them. Heels tap-tap-tapped on the floor and an overhead light flickered and buzzed in unison. I needed silence. I wanted to be home. I needed to be out of there.

'I'm going outside for a cigarette,' I told Tim.

'What if they call you?'

'I don't care. I can't stay in this room.'

Tim knew I would leave if he didn't do something, so he walked over to the nurses' station about thirty feet from the room we were in. I couldn't hear exactly what he was saying, but I heard snatches. *Needs quiet. Autistic. Meltdown. Thank you.*

He came back. 'Come on,' he said, picking up my handbag, 'they say we can wait somewhere quieter.' That somewhere is the room I'm in now, where the sounds are more muted but my nose is assaulted by the smell of antiseptic.

The healthcare assistant comes back and finds me alone. Tim has gone to get some fresh air for a moment. She taps me on the arm. 'I need you to have a shower with this.' She hands me a bottle of medical body wash. 'And you'll need to pop these on.' She puts a hospital gown and a pair of bottle-green compression stockings on the bed.

I can't make the shower the right temperature. It's either too hot or too cold. I can feel the prickly sensation that precedes a meltdown. I can't do this. I want to go home. I fight with the plastic seal on the bottle of body wash. Eventually it yields, scratching my finger as it does so. I sniff the contents. Hospital. Harsh, chemical and frightening.

The throbbing pain from my abscess becomes sharper the longer I stand. I hate my life. I hear a door shut hard and Tim calls my name.

'I'm in the shower,' I say. I have wedged the door slightly open with a towel.

Tim opens the door and looks at me for a minute. I have given up on the shower and am trying to struggle into the compression stockings.

'Phwoar!' he laughs. He is holding a half-eaten Mars bar and a bottle of Evian. It irritates me. A lot. Hunger is one of my main meltdown triggers.

'Fuck off!'

'That's not very nice.'

'Go away.' I say it louder this time, but he ignores me and stands at the window, gazing at the sun setting over the hospital buildings.

Eventually, I win the stockings battle and put the gown on. I can't tie it so ask Tim to help.

'I'm really sorry about this,' I say, a little calmer.

There's a knock on the door and three people come in. They are wearing different-colour scrubs.

'I've come to give you an ECG,' a smiley woman wearing

burgundy says. 'Your notes say you have Ehlers-Danlos syndrome, so we've looked it up and we're worried that the sticky pads might damage your skin.'

I feel reassured. EDS is something many medical professionals are unaware of. I like that she's being honest about not having heard of it and that she has taken the trouble to do some research.

'It'll be fine,' I say. 'My skin isn't fragile. It's just the rest of me that's falling apart.'

She laughs and asks me to undo my gown. Tim hovers in a corner, trying to keep out of the way. He always looks awkward at moments like this, as if he is trying to make himself smaller.

There's another knock on the door and a striking dark-haired woman in navy blue scrubs comes in and introduces herself as the anaesthetist. Tim stands up straighter. He always does this when he sees a woman he finds attractive. I find it endearing. He also makes sure he sounds clever. The anaesthetist walks to the other side of the bed. The room is now feeling very crowded.

This will be my tenth operation in three years. I know the drill. Hours of sitting around feeling hungry and scared, with a sense that nothing will ever happen, the minutes stretching into eternity. Then a sudden burst of activity and a feeling that everything is beginning to move too fast.

'I've just come to have a quick chat about the anaesthetic,' she says.

'I have a routine,' I say. 'As soon as possible, they give me some Midazolam. I also have Fentanyl. I won't have antibiotics, blood thinners or anti-emetics.'

'You have allergies, too. And autonomic dysfunction,' Tim adds, pointlessly.

Someone else comes in. He introduces himself as the surgeon who will be performing my operation. I lean over and grab a piece of paper from the bedside table.

'I've discussed the operation with my consultant and he feels it would be best done like this.'

I hand the paper to the doctor. It has a diagram to show where my abscess is and how the incision should be made.

'I've had a word with him.' He is reassuring and not at all dismissive or argumentative as I imagine he might be. He is short and slight and looks more like a history teacher than someone who cuts open bodies for a living. His hair is thinning and he has delicate metal glasses that look as if they will fall from his nose at any moment. He looks kind. And tired.

This is now going quite well. Before my EDS diagnosis, when my digestive issues and abscesses – this is my fourth – went unexplained or were written off as 'just bad luck', I had my operations in a small private hospital (I was fortunate to have had health insurance). After the EDS diagnosis, I was deemed too much of a risk to be operated on anywhere outside of an NHS general hospital. So I am here, feeling guilty that I am so high-maintenance but also terrified they will give me drugs that will make me even more ill.

Those with EDS are often very sensitive to medications and I haven't found an antibiotic I can tolerate. Any I have taken have caused me to come up in itchy red lines all over my body and to suffer the most appalling upset stomachs, which in turn can lead to some pretty horrific health issues. Once it led to sepsis.

The surgeon takes the sheet of paper from me and studies it.

'Can I examine you?'

'Do you want me to go out?' Tim asks. I find this so strange. He's seen me give birth to two babies.

'I'll just stand over here,' he says moving as far away from the bed as possible. I don't understand his squeamishness. We discussed it after my last op.

'Don't you find it so undignified, being wrapped up like a turkey in a hospital gown and those awful stockings?' he had said.

'A turkey?'

'Well, you know, it's just so undignified.'

I didn't, and still don't, understand what he meant. I don't know what indignity means. Tim says he feels judged by others, but I don't really understand how this feels, what it means and why he cares. We are all here for a reason. I need to be fixed and the doctors get paid to fix me. I don't care what they think of me and imagine they don't care what I think of them. We just need to negotiate a position where we can all get on with playing our roles. Mine to be that of compliant patient. Theirs that of skilful surgeon.

Once it is over and I have readjusted my gown, the doctor gives his verdict. 'It should all be fine, but we won't know exactly what we're dealing with until I can examine you properly once you are under the anaesthetic.'

He looks at my file. 'I see you are refusing antibiotics.'

'Yes. My consultant agrees it's the best course of action and I haven't taken any after my other ops.'

'It's a risk.'

'I know, but I feel I'll be more at risk if I take them.'

I can see he's not thrilled with the situation. He has folded his arms and looks away from me and out of the window.

'You can ring my consultant.'

'No, it's fine. We'll do it your way.'

I sign his consent forms and he leaves. Tim and I are alone again. Suddenly the room feels empty.

Then, there is another knock on the door and a cheery girl comes in.

'Hi. I've come to take you to theatre.'

'What floor is it on?' I ask. 'I can't use lifts.'

For previous operations I have always walked down to theatre and then been given an extra shot of Midazolam just before going back in the lift.

'This floor,' she says. 'Just across the corridor. You can say goodbye to hubby now and you'll be back before you know it.'

119

She takes the brake off my bed and begins to manoeuvre it out of the room.

'It's going to be fine,' Tim says. 'Try not to worry.'

This irritates me hugely. Has he given any thought to the veracity of that statement? How can he possibly know that everything is going to be OK? He has no idea if it will be fine or not. It is beyond annoying when he hands out such platitudes.

The girl driving my bed is too chatty. They always ask the same questions. Do you have children is the opener for women of my age, apparently. I know they do it to take one's mind off what is about to happen, but small talk kills me.

I change the subject. 'How close to death does an anaesthetic actually take one?'

'Ooh, I don't know about that sort of thing,' she says. 'Are your children boys or girls?'

In the pre-theatre anteroom I have to shuffle over from my bed onto the trolley next to me, which is quite a few inches higher.

'How soon can I get the Midazolam?' I ask.

'A couple of minutes,' the beautiful anaesthetist says. Her hair really is very shiny.

'Thank you.' I have to remind myself to be polite. 'Sorry I'm such a pain.'

'You're all right,' she says. 'It's actually rather nice to have a patient with your knowledge of drugs.'

I decide to try again.

'How close to death does an anaesthetic actually take one?'

'It's a very safe procedure,' she says. 'I'm just going to pop a cannula in, so you'll feel a sharp scratch.'

It takes a second and doesn't hurt at all. The room is busy. At least six people are crammed in here.

'Am I your worst patient today?' I ask.

'God no,' she says. 'You don't even come close.'

A man to my right in green scrubs is keen to join the conversation. 'I remember this one patient,' he says, leaning over slightly. 'An elderly patient with dementia. Just as I walked into his room with a cheery hello, the man stood up, walked quickly across the room and said, "I can't believe you'd show your face in here after what you've done," before promptly punching me hard in the face!'

I feel bad for finding it funny and make a mental note to colour in *ashamed*.

'Ready for the Midazolam now?' the anaesthetist asks.

'Yes please.'

She comes towards me, syringe in hand. My heart is beating hard in my chest. I can almost hear it and I can't quite catch my breath. As soon as it takes effect I will be forced to give up controlling everything happening to me.

'You will remember not to give me any antibiotics,' I say as she inserts the needle into the cannula and I begin to feel the cold, sharp sting of the drugs entering my vein.

Then everything becomes calmer. My heart rate slows. I feel an absence of anxiety. The sounds, while they are still there, no longer jar. The lights are still bright, but I am seeing them as if through gauze. Instead of hurting my head they are beautiful. I see the way the light glints off a metal kidney dish and think how pretty it looks. The colours in the room are so vivid. How have I failed to notice them before?

I can hear voices, but can't quite make out what they are saying. It reminds me of being in bed as a child and hearing my parents and their friends talking downstairs over dinner. It's a reassuring sound. One that means I can give up and let someone else take charge for a while.

I lie very still and notice the absence of pain. Everything abrasive is absent. It feels blissful. I squint and look at the lights. They remind me of snowflakes. I look at the blonde ponytail of one of the women in the room. It cascades down her back like a waterfall. It looks as if it would feel soft. I want to reach out and touch it. I hold on to this feeling of everything being OK. It is the neutral I strive for but never quite reach.

Norfolk – Winter 2000

The snow is falling hard now, insulating the world and causing it to fall silent. It is beautiful to watch as it catches in the car's headlights. It is also terrifying.

I can't drive in the snow. Its arrival sends my heart racing. Suddenly the car that is my private space, where I can hide from the world, becomes a dangerous place to be. Familiar landmarks are blanketed in white, making them look different. It's a surreal landscape, one that is unfamiliar.

Even with the merest covering on the road, the rules change and I am gripped with fear. It is too different from what I am used to. I don't know how to react. I grip the steering wheel as if at any moment a patch of invisible ice will send the car into a skid that I will be unable to control.

I pull over to the side of the road and sit with my head in my hands. No one else is out and I am surrounded by blackness. Home feels a world away and as if the territory I would have to cross is hazardous and uncharted.

I wonder when Tim will start to worry. I look at my phone but I have no signal. In my head, I run through my options. Could I walk home from here? *Should* I walk home from here? I am half a mile away, but I don't have a coat with me and my shoes would probably only last five minutes. I could sit it out and wait for service on my phone, then call Tim and get him to pick me up. I check the phone again, but still no bars. There never are on this stretch of the road as it winds its way through dense woodland.

In my rear-view mirror I see a car's headlights in the distance. If I were to pull out just after it passed me, I could follow it and mirror the driver's actions; matching his speed, slowing when he slows, braking when he brakes. Safety in numbers. I switch on the engine and wait, watching the headlights slowly getting bigger and brighter. Then, just as I think it's about to come close, it slowly and deliberately turns off.

I check my pulse. My heart is racing. Another car is approaching. I send a silent prayer into the snowy landscape and it eventually draws level. I pull out behind it and creep along the road. I feel dizzy. I open the window to allow in some fresh air and turn on the radio to feel less alone.

I copy the car's movements and try to remember Tim's advice on driving in the snow. But I'm confused. Is it low gear, high revs or is it the other way round? High gear, low revs?

Eventually, I see the house. I indicate and pull in. I sit on the driveway and switch off the engine. I'm shaking. I look up and Tim is standing by the driver's-side door.

'Hello,' I say, gathering up my things.

'I was worried. I tried to ring, but your phone was just going to voicemail.'

'The journey was a complete nightmare.'

'You could have abandoned it and found a hotel.'

'I wanted to see the children,' I say.

'They're all fast asleep.'

I look at the clock in my car and am surprised to see it's 9 p.m. The children, whose bedtimes are erratic at the best of times, have been staying up later over the past few days. Seeing them would have been a reassurance.

'They were exhausted,' Tim tells me, looking pretty shattered himself.

It's warm in the house. Tim has lit a fire.

'You must be starving?' he says. 'I bought bread and cheese. I thought we could eat in front of the fire. Get you warm.'

'I'm not hungry.' My tone is cold and I can see Tim is hurt. 'Sorry,' I add, 'I just need time to come down a little. You know it takes me time to acclimatize when I've been out for a few days. I just need to get my bearings.'

'Why don't you have a bath and chill out for a bit then?'

'I don't need a bath and it's too early. You know that. I'm going to go into the office and quickly check to see if anyone has emailed. I won't be long.' I start to leave the sitting room before sensing I need to do more. 'Sorry. Just give me half an hour or so. Just to get over this re-entry stage.'

It is close to 10 p.m. when I join Tim again in the sitting room. He switches off the news on TV and we sit on the floor in front of the fire. I look out through the open shutters. The snow is still coming down. I switch on the outside lights and we sit together in silence. It feels as if the world around us is slowly shrinking. There will be no school or nursery tomorrow. Tim will cancel tennis. I will cancel the meeting I am meant to be going to in London.

I can feel the warmth of the fire on my face. I am slowly thawing. Now, it seems as if we are the only people on earth. If every day had the insulating calm of a snow day, I think I could be happy.

I take a piece of bread and cheese and pour a glass of wine. 'I've been thinking about something for a while,' I say. Tim turns to me, suddenly alert.

'I'm not very happy at work. I'm finding it too hard.'

'Hard in what way? I thought you liked it?'

'I do. But I hate the other stuff. The endless meetings. The having to go to the pub after work. The forced team spirit. The three-line-whip on going to the wine bar every Thursday evening. It's so hot and so loud. The people exhaust me. And I think there's something wrong with the building. It makes me feel ill. The lights are too bright and the air is sort of fake. The temperature is all wrong too. I can't concentrate. It's all too loud.

'But also, I just can't cope. I think I should go freelance and work from home. Writing and some PR.'

The statement hangs in the air until a sharp crack from the fire punctures the silence.

'Can we . . . Do you think we can afford to do that?' Tim says. 'Your salary gives us . . . Well, a degree of certainty.'

'I've looked into it,' I say, making an effort to sound confident, 'and I would be able to take some work with me, and I think more would follow.

'I know I would be so much happier not having to go into an office every day. I find it exhausting. I can't cope with people when there are too many of them together in one place. They have strange ideas and weird needs. They talk about someone in unflattering terms one minute and then are cloyingly nice to them the next. It's so disconcerting. You know what it's like. We have endless meetings where nothing seems to happen. Meetings for the sake of it.

'Being at home would be so much better. I would be able to shape my own workplace. Have things where I want them to be.'

'Or lost somewhere in your chaos,' Tim jokes.

'Think about it,' I say, keen not to be distracted. 'There would be no politics to navigate. I would just have to do my best work and everyone would be happy. What would it matter if I didn't get dressed? No one else would know. Just you and me.'

Tim stands up, takes my hand and leads me to the sofa. I put my head in his lap and he strokes my hair. I feel calm.

'I know this is the right thing to do,' I whisper. 'I could be myself.'

CHAPTER EIGHT

June 2016

It is 23 June 2016. The day of Britain's referendum on EU membership and I am at my most stressed. I have been home from hospital for a few weeks and have been starting to feel better. I have been going through my therapy notes, trying to get back on track and going towards allowing more people into my life. After a failed attempt with a personal trainer, I have begun occasionally attending yoga classes held by a friend. I hope to see her more often socially too. She is calming and being with her makes me feel the opposite of jittery.

There are things I haven't managed to do. I can't yet stick to any kind of routine and my self-care skills aren't getting any better. Cleaning my teeth in the morning is hit-and-miss and sometimes at lunchtime I will remember I haven't done it. I rarely brush my hair unless I have to go out to a meeting. I'm not getting outdoors very much at all. Walking the dogs is something I too often leave to Tim. I'm sleeping OK, but haven't been getting dressed every day and haven't been finding time to relax regularly. I still struggle to eat, but usually manage one relatively healthy meal per day. All this causes me to colour in *inadequate*.

My journey towards a better me, however, seems to have been put on hold by my intense interest in the referendum. For weeks I have been researching every aspect of it. Scouring obscure political websites, checking the polling statistics several times each day, joining Facebook groups for each side. While no one else seems prepared even to consider the possibility that Britain may vote to leave, I am convinced – to the core of my very being – that we will. No one will listen to my fears.

Everyone believes the Remain camp will prevail – the pollsters, the bookies, the newspapers, my friends. Everyone. I know they are all wrong and feel sick when I think of the uncertainty leaving the EU would bring. I can't think why anyone would want to vote to leave and am hurt that no one will take my fears seriously. I colour in *confused* and *resentful*. This isn't just about – or even primarily about – a political view. It runs deeper than that. It's about change. I don't remember a time we weren't part of the EU. The idea of not being so is too different for me to be able to contemplate.

It's seven-thirty in the evening and Tim and I are in the sitting room. He is watching the rolling news coverage. I'm pacing the room like a caged animal. We have argued about the likely outcome of the vote and, more acutely, my refusal to think or talk about anything else. He thinks I am panicking about nothing. That there's no hope of Leave winning. Suddenly he gets up from the sofa and turns off the TV with the remote control before throwing it to the floor.

'Right. I'm sorry,' he says, 'but I can't take any more of this. You are obsessing. I know it and I think deep inside you know it too. And it's driving me fucking crazy. You're driving me mad with your endless insistence that you're right – that you know better than the experts – and everybody else is wrong. It's going to be fine and you will have wasted all this time worrying about something that isn't going to happen.'

I'm stung by the venom in his voice. I can't take it when people shout and that discomfort is magnified manifold when Tim loses his temper. It is a raw, animalistic anger.

He regains a little control and his voice softens. 'I'm sorry,' he says, looking straight at me. 'I didn't mean to shout. It's just that we all need a break. Why don't we . . . Let's go out for supper. You need to eat and getting away from the TV and Facebook and bloody Twitter for an hour – just an hour – will do you good.'

I'm fine about this. He's right. I should eat and any of the restaurants we might go to will have Wi-Fi, so I can still keep up with what's going on.

We finally agree to go to the newish Italian in our local town. It's fresh and bright and I am always able to find something I'd like to eat. The staff are good at taking my complicated orders and the Wi-Fi works consistently. I realize these aren't things most people would write in a restaurant review, but they are hugely important to me.

The walls are white, the chairs mismatched and all colours, and the tables are simple wood. It isn't like being in Italy, but it also isn't like being in Norfolk. There's something hopeful about it. Something new, but in a good way.

I sit opposite Tim. Whenever we go out he sits facing towards the restaurant and I sit with my back to it. He likes to see what's going on at all times; I like to feel cut off. Tonight we are the only people in the restaurant. The whole town is pretty dead. I wonder if everyone is planning a long night of watching the coverage live on TV until the result is announced in the early hours. I don't plan to. I am not good without sleep and I am doing a big interview tomorrow. I have to drive from Norfolk to Kent, so will need a good eight hours' sleep.

When I am anxious I cannot eat. It is as if my throat constricts and I cannot easily swallow. As a child I remember sobbing as my parents tried to get me to finish a meal – understandably they were worried I would become ill from being undernourished. Tim gave up trying to get me to eat years ago. He orders a pizza with lots of hot chillies and pepperoni. I try to wade through my pasta. Neither of us can eat. The weather is hot and oppressive. Tonight feels momentous, as if something will be changed forever, yet I am alone in this feeling. Once again I am on the outside.

I am scared. Properly scared. Dealing with change is impossibly hard for me. It takes weeks to accommodate something new into my routine. The coffee shop I go to each day recently stopped selling the blueberry muffins I have each afternoon. Weeks later, I am still trying to get my head around this. If something as seismic as leaving the EU were to happen, I genuinely don't know how I would cope.

Eventually Tim and I give up on eating. I order a latte to take with me and we go home. On the sofa, I begin to shiver, even though it is still bright outside and the sitting room is cloyingly warm. The TV is on and David Dimbleby is summarizing how the next few hours will play out. I flick between Facebook and Twitter, occasionally putting down my phone and staring at the television.

We sit like this for what seems like hours. Tim watching the TV, me glued to Twitter. Occasionally, the boys come down to check on the status of the country's future.

'You're just panicking about nothing,' Toby says. 'It's obvious Remain is going to win.'

'Why is it obvious?' I ask. 'You need to stop believing everything your friends or the news outlets say and start thinking and investigating for yourself. Have you looked around the county? Even in Norfolk, I haven't seen one Remain poster. Literally not one.'

Toby rolls his eyes and looks back at his phone.

I think a part of Tim – the bit that chases danger – is sort of hoping for a Leave win. He'd enjoy the chaos, the drama, the upheaval. It makes me irritated with him. He wasn't really that concerned about the referendum until it became my number one special interest.

'Do you really want Remain to win?' I ask him.

'I just want it to be over. Whatever happens the world won't cave in.'

Nothing annoys me more than people saying 'oh well, the sun will still rise' when something one might regard as appalling is about to happen or has just happened. If we were blasted by nukes, the sun would still rise. If the children fell victim to some terrible accident, the sun would still rise. Why do people say such nonsensical, unhelpful things? If I were worried about the sun failing to rise or the world caving in, then I'm sure these reassurances – if backed up by hardcore facts and scientific evidence – would be helpful. Without these, Tim's comments are mere platitudes.

Then, just after 10 p.m., pictures of Nigel Farage fill the TV screen. He is admitting defeat, his face puffy and red, the bags under his eyes sagging. 'It's been an extraordinary referendum campaign,' he says. 'Turnout looks to be exceptionally high and it looks like Remain will edge it. UKIP and I are going nowhere and the party will only continue to grow stronger in the future.'

I know, as firmly as it is possible to know anything, that he is wrong. That in a few hours he will be popping champagne corks and wondering how he managed to pull this off.

It is a common myth that most people with autism have special skills. That most are savants. That we can name every royal birthday in history or tell you which day of the week any date falls on. In any year. The reality is that 10 per cent of people with autism have savant skills, as opposed to 1 per cent of the general population. That means it is not the case for most of us.

A couple of weeks ago, I called Steve Silberman. He was interesting on the subject of savants and savant-like abilities. He said: 'I think one of the early selling points of autism in pop culture was [the idea of] savant abilities, making it not a disease, but a superpower. I think it engaged hipster imagination.

'I think it is a major misconception that people think either that all autistic people have savant abilities or that they're incredibly rare, as if loads of autistic people are a mess but a few have savant abilities.

'There are some savant abilities that truly are like superpowers, like Stephen Wiltshire's ability to fly over Manhattan for twenty minutes in a helicopter and spend the rest of the week drawing every building there. That's unbelievable, it's amazing. But I think that a sort of lower-level savant ability is actually pretty common. Like autistic people being able to quote long passages of dialogue from their favourite television shows. Or perfect pitch. Those things are not so uncommon.

'The juxtaposition of savant abilities with profound disability was what made it such a fruitful subject for fiction writers in books like *The Curious Incident of the Dog in the Night-Time*. I think there are millions of cultural hooks that make autism interesting to the mainstream.'

I can't even do the most basic of calculations in my head, but I do have one skill that I have honed over the years, although it is still far from being anything like a savant's. I can spot patterns. I can take a few pieces of information and build the whole picture. And I can tell when something will become popular or a trend. I have never been wrong.

I don't know how or why I can do this and it certainly isn't based on any mathematical logic. It's more a feeling, like taking the temperature of a situation and being able to see what the outcome will be. I think it's partly because I work from a place of logic, rather than emotion. While most Remain supporters *believed* their side would win (because how could it not happen, how could others not make the right choice?), I *knew* Remain would lose.

Everyone else seemed to exist in their own echo chambers, on social media following mainstream media outlets that backed up their own views. By contrast, I tried to engage with people with very different views to mine. I talked to Leave voters. I looked at the evidence. I saw disparate groups of people coming together and voting for a host of different reasons. I visited the UKIP Facebook pages and those of the prominent Leave campaigners and studied the conversations going on. I saw the different views. I saw the passion. I argued with those whose views were alien to me. And it became clear to me, in the weeks running up to the vote, that it would be almost impossible for Leave to lose.

There was a moment when the tide could have turned. The day the reprehensible Leave campaign poster was unveiled showing streams of refugees under the headline *Breaking point: why the EU has failed us*. June 16th. The same day the Labour MP Jo Cox was killed. It was as if there was a momentary pause, a collective deep breath. Campaigning stopped, the conversations didn't. But just for a short while the tone changed slightly and there was the possibility things could turn out differently.

That didn't happen and, as I watch the results slowly trickle in, I know the world – my world – is going to be a very different place.

My heart races and I cannot remain calm. I'm under a blanket on the sofa. Every half an hour or so, I tell Tim I will be going to bed in ten minutes. I don't. I am compelled to keep looking at the screen. It is like watching a car crash over and over.

Jack and his girlfriend, Mary, arrive home and say hi, but then go to their room. Tim and I sit together watching the coverage on the BBC and occasionally channel-hopping to see how other broadcasters are reporting events. The TV screen fills with a graphic showing the value of the pound plummeting in an almost perfect vertical line.

Jack bursts in, showing us the same graphic on his phone. 'Have you seen the pound!'

I can't bear to look at the TV. The Twitter app is open on my phone, the Facebook app on my iPad. I flick from one to the other, while the commentary from David Dimbleby continues in the background. His voice is mesmerizing. I remember it from childhood. It has such an air of calm authority that it makes me feel as if, come what may, there are still some grown-ups around.

Toby and Mary drift downstairs to join us, our faces silver from the screen in the corner.

'What will happen if Scotland votes to stay and England to leave?' Jack asks.

'I don't know,' Tim says.

'What if it's too close to call?' Toby asks.

'I don't know.'

'If we do vote to leave, when would it happen?' Jack asks.

'I don't know. No one knows. It's all uncharted territory.'

The questions continue and we have to keep repeating that we just don't know. It seems as if tonight we don't have many answers. I go upstairs to bed, but find myself compelled to get up within five or ten minutes. I can't sleep. The sitting room has a magnetic pull on me. Watching this unfold on Twitter in bed, alone, feels wrong somehow.

I chat on Facebook to those friends who are still up. Somewhere deep in the darkness, author and journalist India Knight tweets: *I think we may be fucked. Plus side: I know nothing.*

I reply: *But your earlier cautious optimism was keeping me going.*

She says: *It wasn't even cautious* :(

I go upstairs again. I come down again. Repeating the pattern over and over. I have a feeling radiating through my chest and stomach that I can't quite describe, a churning. Fear plus. I feel very cold. Now I understand what *cold* means on the feelings wheel. I colour it in. Dark blue.

Then it comes. Dimbleby – his face drawn, his eyes tired and resigned – announces what others had begun to fear but I long knew for certain.

'Well, at twenty minutes to five,' he says, 'we can now say the decision taken in 1975 by this country to join the Common Market has been reversed by this referendum to leave the EU.'

'This is mad,' Jack says. Mary looks pale and worried as she sits on the edge of the sofa, occupying as little space as possible. Toby looks unsure of what to make of it. Tim is silent. I look at my phone.

The food writer William Sitwell has tweeted: *We're out, says Dimbleby. Shan't forget that moment.*

I know those words will stay implanted on my brain, repeating themselves over and over in the way snatches of poetry or song lyrics do. I find I am crying. I never cry. It's not that I don't want to, it just doesn't happen. Usually I stay frozen. It feels strange and good and strange and bad.

The boys and Mary are now asleep. Tim decides to go to bed to catch a couple of hours. On Twitter, Rachael Lucas, one of the only other autistic women I have dared to strike up an online relationship with, says: *I don't want to tell my children – who said at the polling station 'it'll be OK, won't it?'– that no, it won't be.*

I reply: *My heart breaks for all our children.*

She says: *My smallest doesn't understand why anyone would want to leave. My older ones want to know why they don't have a say.*

Mine did have a say. It was the first time the boys had been able to vote and it was one of those moments when I realized I was now the mother of young adults. Tim took a picture of them and sent it to me. The polling station in a church in a neighbouring village is so pretty. The boys are standing outside the gates. In the picture they look carefree. Jack is wearing an awful green and orange Hawaiian-patterned shirt with blue shorts and Green Flash tennis shoes. Toby is, as ever, dressed head to toe in black. Mary is standing in the background, looking elegant and slightly apart from these puppy-like boys who are all long limbs and big eyes. Her blonde hair is poker straight, her posture perfect.

They are about to go in and cast their vote, these almost men. It's another step on the road to adulthood and away from the life of their childhood that I am clinging to with increasing desperation. I love the picture. I made it the screensaver on my phone.

My experience of motherhood is, I think, in many ways different to that of neurotypical women. As well as not recognizing my own emotions and feeling them at a very muted level, I don't cope well with the emotions of others. I would like to live in a world where we all went along on a straight emotional line, never feeling anything too strongly.

Because of this, I cannot bear for my children to feel upset or disappointed. Their pain, however minor, is always simply too much for me to cope with, so I do everything I can to not allow them to suffer any negative emotions. I guess in today's terms I would be called a *snowplough mother* as I clear all obstacles from their paths.

This time there was nothing I could do and I knew they would be upset. I feel a weird guilt, as if somehow there must have been something I could have done. Maybe I could have voted harder somehow, made it count more.

At 07.17 I get a message from Lucie. *I am so sad. I woke up at 4 a.m. and checked.* In the end I decide to go in to the boys and Mary at 7.30 a.m. Jack wakes like a confused puppy, stretching. Mary, seemingly sensing bad news, sits bolt upright. 'Oh god, this is bad.'

When I go to Toby's room, he turns over and looks at me. 'I said you would cry.'

Norfolk – Spring 2002

'Which carriage will we sit in?' Toby asks. 'Annie or Clarabel?'

The boys are excited. They've been talking about it for weeks. A trip on a steam train. The real-life Thomas the Tank Engine.

'Annie!' Jack says. At six, a year older than Toby, he revels in a sense of authority, but he looks to me as he always does to reassure him that he is right.

'I don't know,' I say. 'Let's wait and see.'

It is half-term and I am enjoying the break. It is not too short, not too long. It is a punctuation mark in the sentence that is real life. It is as if the world has stopped for a while, frozen in time on the platform of a rural station that looks unchanged since the 1950s.

'Will the carriages really be the same as they are on Thomas?' Lucie asks in a quiet voice so the boys don't hear.

'They're going to be disappointed if they're not exactly what they're expecting.'

I shrug. 'I'm sure they'll love it whatever the carriage is like.' I hope I'm right.

The station is crowded, alive with the chatter of children. We wait in an isolated huddle at the far end of the platform. Part of the throng, but separate from it. The boys' hands squirm in mine.

I see the train in the distance and Tatti notices it at the exact moment I do. She squeals and jumps up and down on the spot, her hair flying around her face. Her excitement is contagious and I struggle to hold on to the boys.

'You have to hold Mummy's hand,' Lucie says. 'It might be dangerous if you don't.' She is only twelve, but she seems more of a grown-up every day. She has a maturity beyond her years, a gentle, quiet confidence.

Jack stands very still, his eyes fixed and bright, as the train lurches into the station, its front adorned with a giant smiling face.

'It's really Thomas,' he whispers, his voice taking on the babyish tone it does when he is excited or unsure. Jack worries in a way not shared by any of the other children, his enthusiasm always tinged with apprehension. He takes longer to process the world than others of his age and needs to see how they are experiencing something before he is entirely comfortable. He will let his younger brother climb a tree first. Will he reach the top or will he fall and break his arm?

Toby is more his own person. He knows what he likes and what he does not. If he tires of a walk, he will sit down and refuse to get up. If he doesn't like the look of something on his plate he will refuse to eat it. He wriggles next to me, impatient to get on board. Impatient for an adventure.

Tim joins us carrying biscuits and cartons of juice and we board the train. The sweet smells of steam, wood and aged upholstery fill the air. It's as if we have travelled back in time, back to *The Railway Children*, *Carrie's War* or *The Children of*

Green Knowe. The girls love it too. It is romantic, old-fashioned and reminiscent of the books we share a love of.

We make our way down the carriage and find our seats. There's a flurry of coats being unzipped and drinks being handed out. There is a loud clunk as the train lumbers into life, slowly moving forward, then gradually building up a head of steam.

The view from the train as it hugs the North Norfolk coastline provides a new perspective on a familiar world. The beaches where we build sandcastles for Ziggy to knock down in his clumsy exuberance. The ice-cream shop where the girls order sensible ice lollies and Jack and Toby load cones with four flavours and mountains of sprinkles and marshmallow chunks. The fifty-metre-high viewing platform where Toby rushes to the top to see if he can see our house and where Jack slowly climbs up, stopping to check the height from the ground at every step.

The view is timeless – trees, a windmill, a glimpse of the sea. I wonder what it must have been like when this was a proper train route, rather than one for children and tourists. I try to imagine living in the 1950s. I think life would be easier. I think maybe I would have liked being a housewife with nothing to think of but domesticity. I am not great at cleaning, but I do love cooking and am in the middle of writing a cookery book. I wish it were possible actually to travel back in time. I have been reading about time slips and revisiting childhood books such as *Come Back Lucy* and *Charlotte Sometimes*. How amazing it would be to stray into the wrong time. How liberating. I lose myself for a moment in the possibility of it all.

The children are sharing a table of four, Tim and I sitting on the other side of the aisle. Jack gets up from his seat and puts his head in my lap. I begin to stroke it, in time with the rhythm of the train. His hair feels slightly coarser than it did a year or so ago. It is a sign he is growing up. I feel a pang. I like the baby days best.

The train lets out a loud *choo-choo* and clouds of steam drift past the window.

'Ghosts,' Jack cries, excitement in his voice. 'Look! Ghosts!'

'Look, Diddut, we're higher than the trees,' Toby shouts, holding his stuffed rabbit to the window. 'We're flying.'

Lucie says something I don't catch and Toby starts giggling. It's a deep, throaty chuckle and it is infectious. Jack leaps up and goes back to his seat, afraid he is missing out on something.

Tatti's face is the picture of concentration as she bends over her colouring book, trying hard to keep within the lines even though the speed of the train is causing her to bounce in her seat. Lucie gives Toby an indulgent look (as if he is being so childish) and returns to her Game Boy.

A certain peace settles, the children lost in their own worlds. The gentle, reassuring rumble of the train providing a hypnotic soundtrack. Tim and I talk about plans for the weekend. Tonight we will take the children for fish and chips on the pier. Tomorrow we will go for a walk in the country park.

Then it will be Monday and back to work for us and school for the children. Back to the real world. I feel a jolt of anxiety shoot through me. I want to stay insulated by the cosy feeling of the holidays. I don't want to go back to reality.

As if he has read my mind, Jack leans across the aisle, his eyes watery.

'I don't want to go to school on Monday.'

'OK,' I say. 'You don't have to.'

Tim turns his gaze away from the ribbons of sand and sea skipping past.

'You can't keep letting them not go to school, just because they don't fancy it.' His tone is hushed but harsh.

'He's six,' I reply. 'What's he going to miss? Trigonometry?'

'That's not the point. You can't keep giving in to them and allowing them to get their own way all the time.'

'Why not?' I say, meaning it.

I don't understand why people impose so many rules on

their children. I hated the lack of control I felt throughout my childhood and I don't want to impose it on the people I love most. They seem too small, too fragile to have to cope with pain and disappointment. I find it agonizing to watch their faces crease with sadness or to see tears roll down their cheeks.

'You're being ridiculous,' Tim replies, but not unkindly.

The children watch us with interest. Not upset by the exchange. Interested.

'I didn't learn anything at school,' I say airily.

'Well everyone's not you. We have a responsibility. A legal responsibility, but also a responsibility as parents.'

I hate having to force the children to go to school, to do something I found almost unbearable. Jack likes it least and is the one who most often tries to wheedle a day off. I don't mind at all. I understand.

We pass a field of sheep and my reverie is interrupted by the children chorusing a loud *baaah!* Lucie does a very good impression of a sheep and the boys make her do it again and again. Tim and I join in until our animal noises fill the carriage and the tension drifts off into the steam.

'I just hate forcing them to do something they don't want to,' I say.

'OK,' he says, with a sigh of resignation, 'but this is the last time.'

CHAPTER NINE

July 2016

The Brexit vote has changed things at home. For the first time in my life I am worried I may be properly depressed. I have sunk into a dark space and don't know how to climb out. The days stretch into one another and I am tearful and panicky. I can't understand how the rest of the world is functioning.

Tim is at the end of his tether and has imposed a moratorium on discussing politics. He says my obsession – my ceaseless questioning, my endless time spent on social media and my unending need to debate every aspect of the referendum vote and its likely effects on our future – is causing friction between us. I think he believes that if he won't engage on the subject I'll forget about it.

I will walk into a room and say something like, 'It looks as if Andrea Leadsom is going to step out of the leadership contest,' and he jokingly holds up his hand like a traffic policeman. He does it with affection, but he has had enough and the stress is showing. He is exhausted, worn down, slightly erased somehow.

I don't forget about it. I find other people to talk to, online, late into the night. It makes me feel separate from him. I focus on looking back on my life to try to make sense of where I am now. And forward into a future in a country I no longer recognize as my own. I ignore all that is happening now, in the present. Tim can only exist in the present. The past is gone for him and the future too distant to contemplate. The gulf between us seems vast.

Marriage is hard. Alexandre Dumas wrote: *The chain of marriage is so heavy that it takes two to bear it; sometimes three.* For me, it is more like thirty. I need a number of people to talk and listen to me as I try to make sense of the world. I collect people online, those willing to analyse, debate, discuss and console. I like these types of friendship. They don't ask too much of me. There's a shared interest, but if one of us wanders off and on to something new it really doesn't matter. There are plenty of other people willing to talk.

I start visiting pro-Brexit pages and this leads me into the murky world of far right, alt-right and extremist groups online. Their words of hate and bigotry are abhorrent, their spelling and grammar those of a five-year-old. Many are old ladies. It shocks me. Rocks my belief that ultimately we are all good people, just doing our best to get by. I feel obliged to step in, to post comments whenever I see vile racism and ignorant untruths.

Tony Attwood believes there is logic behind my intense interest when I tell him I need to understand the points of view of the most hardcore Leave voters. He told me: 'You've hit the nail on the head. You're trying to understand the motives of people and – if you're not good at getting into the minds of people and understanding them – then the special interest is a way of exploring your concern.

'All special interests serve a function. It may be a sense of self-worth or a sense of identity because, if you're good at Minecraft, then you're valuable at school. And sometimes the interest can become a source of employment. There are a variety of reasons why the special interest is valuable for emotion management and also emotional understanding of the thoughts and feelings of other people. It is a thought blocker, a refresher. It gives you a sense of comfort and enjoyment and it's what I call an intellectual orgasm.

'I think in many ways neurotypicals don't appreciate or need an interest, so they assume an autistic person doesn't need one. But I have an issue when parents focus on special interests as discipline. If the child is not doing what the parents want them to, they will punish the child by taking away a special interest. I don't call that punishment. I call it revenge. When they do that they are not giving the child a replacement for the value of that interest in their life and that's counterproductive.

'When you look at special interests, there are many reasons for them. First of all, the person really enjoys and is comforted by facts and information. Facts and information are comforting, but they also build up your own self-esteem and sense of self-worth. If you're not good socially and you're not good at sport, for example, the one thing you can be good at is knowledge.'

Brexit is an obsession, but unlike any other I've ever had. It could not be described as a special interest. This is negative. It is destructive. It is futile and it is dangerous. I am bombarded by threats from men whose behaviour raises so many red flags it practically turns the screen of my phone crimson.

I could write here the things I have read, but I don't want to. They require a trigger warning. These people don't deserve the airtime. Women are threatened and abused online every day. It is a sad indictment of where we are now. I was never afraid but I was shocked to my core that people think the way they do.

Somehow I keep going, trying to talk sense into this weird, disparate bunch of people whose hatred is corrosive. Late into the night I read things that make me want to weep with anger and frustration. There's a line from Aaron Sorkin's TV drama *The Newsroom* that talks of *speaking truth to stupid*. It's what I'm doing but I just can't stop.

I text a friend and give him a watered-down version of a recent hate-filled comment. *It's pointless*, he replies. *You'll never change their minds.*

I have such a problem with people spouting opinion as fact. It is an almost physical pain. Facts are so important. Facts are my friends. I have been collecting them since I was at primary school. They make me feel safe. A fact is irrefutable. It cannot be challenged if there's enough evidence to back it up. Except that these people do challenge.

They believe in conspiracy theories. Any story they don't like has been invented by a liberal media elite. Any they support are utterly true, however unlikely they sound. It hurts my head. Some of my friends see my comments on Facebook and follow me into these groups. They try to make sense of it too. When they can't, they quickly leave and block the page. I wish I could do that. I wish I could accept that some people think differently to me, but there's a small part of my brain that believes if you throw enough facts at someone they will change their view, however firmly held.

The need to convince someone they are wrong – when one has irrefutable evidence – is not an exclusively autistic trait. Many feel this way, but autistic people tend to try for longer than the vast majority of neurotypical people would.

A friend tells me how every year she and her family would visit the same B&B in rural Ireland. The owner's autistic son had a special interest in trains. Each year, he would have collected more images and information and would be at the door, waiting for them with his folder of evidence in hand. She still occasionally goes back and it's still happening, more than twenty years later. The boy, now a man, feels compelled to share every aspect of his interest. I'm like this with facts. I feel compelled to tell people when they have got something factually incorrect or, worse still, when they are sharing articles with absolutely no basis in truth.

I have never learned how to break an obsession. I have never had to. In most cases a new one comes along, takes over from the last and replaces it. When we were in our twenties, some of my friends got over one boyfriend by getting under another. I'm like this with obsessions. The previous one needs a new one to replace it. Otherwise it will just go on.

I want so much to stop worrying about the future, about the divide in the country and about the fact that no one seems to have a bloody clue what's going on. I am trying to stay away from the far-right groups. They are making me unhappy, unproductive and frightened. Like a dysfunctional relationship, they are difficult to quit.

I decide to try the Twelve Steps one-day-at-a-time approach, but working in blocks of minutes rather than days. I resolve to finish a feature before I am 'allowed' to go back online. I'll tell myself to pop out and get a coffee, instead of logging back on to Facebook. I will take baths, message someone nice, eat chocolate. Anything to keep away from the dark corners of the internet where it's impossible to find any alternative to hate.

CHAPTER TEN

August 2016

A new focus creeps into my life. A new question forms in my mind. Why am I autistic? It's a complicated and controversial subject. Many autistic adults believe that too much investigation into the causes of autism will, ultimately, lead to eugenics. If science discovers the genes that cause autism, screening tests will become available and parents may be advised to end pregnancies. Essentially autistic people could be weeded out of society.

This would be a terrifying outcome. Autistic people bring so much to the world. We are scientists and artists, writers and doctors. We are gardeners and primary school teachers. Council workers and cleaners. But more than this, we are human with the same hopes and fears and dreams and desires as everyone else.

Instead of an endless search for a cause, many autistic people feel – rightly, I believe – that money should be spent on finding ways to support children and adults on the spectrum. Education and employment should be made more accessible and inclusive.

While I wholeheartedly agree with all of this, something in my make-up means I need answers to everything. I don't want to know why autism occurs per se. I just want to know where my autism began, how it has shaped my life and what would have been different had I been born neurotypical.

I talk to Steve Silberman. His book, *Neurotribes*, is the most comprehensive work on the subject. He wrote a piece on autism for *Wired* magazine and became massively interested.

Although he is not on the spectrum himself, he gave over five years of his life to researching and writing the book.

I ask what fired his interest.

'I saw the inability to answer the question as to why the number of diagnoses has spiked so dramatically,' he says, 'starting in the early 1990s. I saw autism perpetually described in the media as a mystery, an enigma, a puzzle. That lack of explanation was causing a tremendous amount of human suffering. I saw there was a panorama of human suffering with everyone asking why. What could be more terrifying for parents than that autism was an epidemic?'

This is an interesting point. Parents can, understandably, be terrified at the idea of their child being diagnosed with autism when there is so much misinformation out there. With changes in the diagnostic criteria, better screening and more awareness, rates of diagnosis are thankfully going up. That doesn't mean there are more autistic people than ever, but that more are being noticed and getting the support they deserve.

Steve Silberman's book and subsequent interviews have done a lot to address the positive side of autism, as well as to debunk many of the myths.

He adds: 'There are millions of memes on the internet showing the dramatic rise in diagnosis and those memes have been perpetuated by groups. The most trusted sources of information in the parent community are calling autism not just an epidemic, but an epidemic that poses a greater threat to children than paediatric AIDS or diabetes. They literally used that. They literally used paediatric AIDs, cancer and diabetes as the equivalent or worse.

'I wanted to correct the misconception that autism is an epidemic. Another was that autistic people are less than human. That they don't experience the whole range of human emotions, human hopes, human wishes and desires. In earlier descriptions, autistic people are nothing but a list of impairments and deficits and that was something I wanted to put right. I could not possibly write about autistic people in the shallow or stereotypical ways that we see so much of. It was so obvious to me that they are deep and complicated, nuanced and passionate and funny.'

While there are so many more people getting diagnosed, it is still harder for women and girls to get the attention they deserve. According to the UK's National Autistic Society, various studies – together with anecdotal evidence – have arrived at men/women ratios ranging from 2:1 to 16:1.

Sarah Wild, head of Limpsfield Grange, agrees it's an issue. She told me: 'Making people aware that girls can have autism is still a massive challenge. People still judge girls by the male criteria, so it feels as if they doubly don't fit in. They don't fit into neurotypical norms, but they also don't fit into everyone else's construct of what autism is.

'We place a strong emphasis on staying well, long term. The girls here are amazing and I think they can do anything they want to do. The one thing that stops them is life becoming a bit unpredictable, which can sometimes make them unwell. There's not very much awareness of female autism and there is even less awareness of female autism plus mental health difficulties. I think they don't get the right support.'

I feel lucky to have been diagnosed at a time when there is much more awareness. It's important to differentiate, however, between awareness and understanding. Many people dismiss autistic women, simply because they do not fit the stereotypical version of autism that society is used to seeing.

I mention this to Steve Silberman, who laughs. 'Oh yeah and, knowing neurotypicals, they'll say *you don't seem autistic* and expect you to take it as a compliment. I don't mean to equate these things, but I'm gay and, when I was growing up, people would often say to me when I came out to them, *well, you don't seem gay to me* and it's a rather bitter compliment to absorb.'

Whenever I thought about autism before my diagnosis, I really would imagine the geeky guy from IT who wouldn't get jokes or be able to hold a conversation. Since my diagnosis, though, I have encountered hundreds of autistic people and every one is as different as we would expect neurotypical people to be.

Before I became interested in the subject, I believed that the spectrum meant that at one end there were the very autistic people; at the other the mildly autistic. Many lovely, well-meaning neurotypical people find the idea of autism really tricky to grasp. They think, because of my job, marriage and children, that I am 'only a little bit autistic'. 'You're obviously very low on the spectrum' is something else I hear a lot.

That the spectrum is linear couldn't be further from the truth. To get a more accurate perspective I met Dr Judith Gould at the Lorna Wing Centre for Autism. Judith is a chartered consultant clinical psychologist with more than forty years' experience. She specializes in autism spectrum disorders and learning disabilities. In the 1970s, with the late Dr Lorna Wing, Judith came up with the term autism spectrum.

Judith believes the key point to understand is that autism is a spectrum not because it is linear but because any factor can be present at any point. She said: '[In our study] we saw the classic autistic aloof person with repetitive rituals and elaborate routines. But we also saw children with aspects of social difficulties, communication difficulties and imagination difficulties who didn't fit in with [earlier] precise criteria.

'These traits tended to be seen together, but you could have anything on the dimension. Anything on the communication dimension, anything on the imagination dimension and so on. At first we called it the autism continuum. Continuum implied severity from high to low but that's not what we meant. The spectrum would look like a rainbow because anything can happen at any point. The colours merge.

'In terms of communication, people can come anywhere on the spectrum. There are those who only communicate their needs and there are those who don't realize the person they are with may be getting bored when they talk about special interests. Then you've got those with a highly intellectual, formal, little professor communication style.

'Then there is imagination. You've got those children or adults with no imaginative activities. No play. Then there are those who copy – and they're often the girls. So a child is playing with a doll, bathing a doll, and another little girl is sitting beside her, copying. But what she does is put the head of the doll *in* the water. So the symbolic baby isn't there, but the actions look alike.

'One of my favourite examples comes from the early days. I was assessing a child and Lorna was taking the developmental history. The boy set up this incredible scene with a train set, some Play-Doh and little characters he made out of Lego people. I reported back to his mother that he had shown amazing imaginative play, but when I described what he had done she pointed out he had, in fact, created an exact replica of what he had seen on one of his *Thomas the Tank Engine* DVDs. So my message here, which we give to psychologists, is if you're seeing a child in a one-to-one situation and you're observing play, don't necessarily accept that it is real imaginative play.

'Then you've got those with imaginative play that is repetitive and stereotyped. Right up the top here we have those people who create their own fantasy worlds with amazing creativity but it is not social creativity. So some people are very creative, but when it comes to understanding consequences of actions, they keep repeating the same mistakes and getting into trouble.

'Unfortunately, I don't think people can easily recognize repetitive rigidity behaviour in very bright people. They've got fascinating interests they can talk to you about and they can create music, art, science, IT and so on. They're brilliant. So, if you don't ask the right questions, you'll say they're flexible.'

Since I got my diagnosis, I can't help but ask the *why am I autistic* question. Dr Judith Gould stresses that it is a combination of genes and environment. She told me: 'There are lots of autisms. We now know it is a genetic condition. So, when assessing people, I ask about other family members. Often they won't know the person is autistic so I will ask if there's anyone in the family who may be very successful but is rather unusual or different. So, in answer to your question, we don't really know why you are autistic, but we do know that there is a high genetic component. However, it is not a straightforward component.'

'I've read in so many places that it's genetic and environmental,' I said, 'but I'm not sure I understand exactly what environmental means in this context?'

'Well, I think it means you have the predisposition to behave in the way we've described the autistic pattern of behaviour to be, but your environment will also impact on that. Whether you are in a very structured environment. Whether people are aware and recognize your differences and support you; then, maybe, you may not ever need to have a diagnosis.

'In my clinical experience, most people on the autism spectrum have sensory issues. Either hyper- or hypo-sensitive. If you're in an environment that impacts in a sensory way and makes you overloaded, you will respond and make it more obvious that there is a difficulty. Sensory issues will depend very much on where you're brought up and how knowledgeable people are as to how your symptoms will develop. But essentially the autism will be there.'

On an intellectual level, this makes perfect sense. I was always going to be autistic and – unless I lived in an environment that didn't impact on me at all – it was always going to be a major factor in my life.

My diagnosis helped me make sense of so many things in my life, including my inflexibility and sensory issues, so it has been hugely useful for me. I remember, though, asking Dr Kajee whether everyone feels positively about being diagnosed.

She told me: 'I think it depends on the individual. One of the questions in our diagnostic interviews is *why do you want the diagnosis and how do you feel it will help you?* So I always try when I'm seeing somebody to get that sense from them.

'Some people like labels, some people don't and I think it depends on where you are in your life and how you feel. I know you found it immensely helpful because it helped you place a lot of things into context. I suppose you wouldn't really understand why some people wouldn't want a diagnosis. It would completely befuddle you because it has been positive for you. You wouldn't be able to see how it could be negative for someone else.

'I guess some people feel they don't want to be known as the label. They come from a different perspective and just feel they don't want to know. They don't want to be categorized. They'd rather be seen as odd or eccentric or different. But most people who come to see me, on some level want that clarity, that peace of mind.'

Tim and I are sitting in the garden. I'm reading a paper on autism; he's halfway through the crossword. We have no plans. The sun is warm and usually at this time of year we would be thinking about a holiday. This year we're not. Money is tighter than usual and I can't contemplate going away when the time left with the children is so limited.

'We could find somewhere cheap to go,' Tim says, a wheedling note creeping into his voice.

I thought the holiday conversation was over and I wasn't planning on talking about it now. I tell him I want to do some more research into autism. I say I'm planning to write more on the subject and maybe it would be a good time to do it over the next month or so when things look as if they will be quieter.

'Why can't you just accept what is?' he says later. 'You did say that once you had a firm diagnosis you would stop allowing it to dominate your life.'

Irritation is creasing his brow. Washing-up is piled high in the sink and I feel guilty that I'm leaving him to take care of the domestic stuff. I look at the wrinkles on his forehead and wonder how many of them I have put there. He is an idealist, an optimist. He wants a life filled with excitement and contentment. He cannot see the two are as incompatible as oil and water.

He wants parts of me, but not all of me. He cannot understand, even after twenty years of marriage, that I am not going to change. I am a realist. I can take the good parts of someone and ignore the rest. I don't think I get as bound up in relationships as non-autistic people. If I get irritated by something I either remove myself from the situation or politely raise the subject.

I don't do drama. I can't have a screaming row. It feels wrong and destabilizing. I can't even defend myself if I am wrongly accused. I will do anything to keep things quiet and stable.

On an intellectual level, I understand that compromise is meant to be at the heart of relationships, that we are meant to come together as one in a way that accommodates our differences. On an emotional level, however, all I feel is *how is this even possible?*

I wish I could be the wife Tim wants me to be. The one who will agree to learn to tango on a whim or will say, let's chuck it all in and go on a grown-up gap year. But my need for stability – to keep working, to keep my day-to-day the same – doesn't allow for that kind of huge change. I don't do spontaneity.

I worry I have done to him what I most fear someone might do to me. That I have subsumed him. Stopped him from being him. I feel sick at the thought of it. Have I unwittingly done this? Rationalizing it, I know I have encouraged him to follow his dreams. To find a way to visit Norway to see the aurora borealis. To photograph polar bears in Spitsbergen. To follow prides of lions in the Serengeti.

Perhaps I am the excuse he needs not to do such things. Perhaps telling himself that he cannot do these things because of me – even with firm evidence to the contrary – saves him from having to face up to his own shortcomings; by his own admission he lacks drive and ambition. I ask him to give me his perspective.

'You haven't subsumed me in any way,' he says. 'If anything you have sacrificed too much of yourself for me. If I bombard you with stuff to do – to see the Northern Lights, to visit Alaska, whatever – it's because I'm desperate to share everything with you. To see you experience real enjoyment, to see you let yourself go and just live in the moment. With your guard down.'

The sentiment is lovely, but it is also quintessentially neurotypical. It is faulty thinking to believe that because he is interested in something, I will be too. This has been happening to me with neurotypicals since I was a small child. It began with food. *Just try these fish fingers. You'll like this cheese sandwich. Give this new brand of cereal a go – you'll love it.* As I grew older, it became: *Come to this party, meet this new person, try this new job.*

It takes a while to accommodate anything new into my life and it's better if it slowly finds its way in. When something new happens, it knocks me off balance. It makes me question the other parts of my routine. A friend, Mark, once told me that many of his romantic relationships ended due to his *non-attendance*. I'm like this with too many things in my life.

Instead of looking outwards, or taking in the interests of others, I focus on my special interests. They can be subjects as diverse as the psychology behind school shootings, politics, a particular clothing brand, a movie or a book. I can become fascinated by an historical event, such as the hours after Kennedy's assassination. I can find I suddenly need to learn everything there is to know about etiquette in the 1950s or a particular style of cooking.

For me, a special interest takes the form of needing to know everything possible on the subject. The world we live in is messy, complicated, loud, painful, and makes little sense. My special interests keep me safe. They stop my anxiety from spinning out of control. They ground me. I find facts about them in books, online or in other people's heads. These facts are soothing and I layer one upon another until they have the effect of a balm.

If my interests were people-focused, they would be too painful to deal with. People are unpredictable. They say one thing and mean another. They tell you things you want to hear, rather than the truth. Autistic honesty has a purity. Ask us a question and we will tell you the truth. One hundred per cent. Undiluted by squeamishness. Unadulterated.

Of course, I have learned to lie socially. If someone asks what I think of her new haircut and it looks awful, I can say I like it. I can't, however, resist the urge to add some truthful reflection, such as, 'Have you thought about wearing it back off your forehead?' or, 'Maybe if you had the back cut a little shorter it would make you feel less conscious of it.' I have to find a solution to a problem. If I'd just said, 'Wow, it looks awesome,' would she have felt better? Probably. But for how long? Surely people don't believe the lies they are told all day.

I look for characters on TV and in movies who might be autistic. Not the typical, geeky males, but subtler female types. I think we all need to see ourselves represented. Many raise the character of Saga Norén (played by Sofia Helin) in the Swedish/Danish television drama *The Bridge*, but I don't relate that much to her. I find her too dark. Where I do feel a synergy is with Elise Wassermann (Clémence Poésy) in the English/French version, *The Tunnel*. She is much more like me when I am not pretending.

However, the TV character I relate to most is Sloan Sabbith (Olivia Munn), in *The Newsroom*. I'm not sure she is written to be autistic, but she's good at her job despite social skills that are wonky. She manages to have relationships of sorts, but they are tricky and dysfunctional. She's absorbed by her subject – financial news – and, although I know literally nothing about this, I am very much reminded of myself when she talks about her specialist subject. She reels off facts about the debt ceiling in a way that seems more than professional. Instead, it seems like a passion. It reminds me of the way I talk about whatever is occupying my brain.

Most autistic women and girls – whether diagnosed or not – seem naturally and inherently to find a way to copy their neurotypical peers, be they girls in their class, colleagues or even characters in books or on screen. *The Newsroom* also provides me with a role model to copy – MacKenzie McHale, played by Emily Mortimer. She is pretty much perfect. She is passionate, but not obsessive. She is devoted to her work but has outside interests. She is not afraid to show her emotions. She makes mistakes and survives.

The sun goes behind a cloud and I ask Tim if he wants to go inside. We go into the kitchen and I suggest I make some chicken burgers. He sits at the table still doing the crossword while I line up the ingredients.

'What about my autism do you find annoying?' I ask.

'Really? Again?'

'I want to know. Give me anything.'

'You know I hate doing this, but – oh, I don't know – you wear the same clothes every day. Jeans and a grey T-shirt or jumper. You have no concept of dressing for anyone but yourself.'

I think about this. It's true, but I am confused at the idea of dressing for someone else. It makes little sense to me. Clothes need to be comfortable and liveable with. I cannot stand anything patterned. Jack does a good line in very loud, hipster shirts, which I can barely stand to look at. The patterns make me feel vertiginous, as if I might faint. Generally most of my clothes are black, white, grey or dark blue. I endlessly buy very similar soft, grey sweaters.

I tend to shop only in one place at any given time because shopping is not an experience I enjoy. I buy good clothes, designed to last, and couldn't contemplate facing a Saturday on the high street. That people do it weekly, as if it were a hobby, is such an alien concept to me.

'I'd like to see you in something different,' he says.

I cannot understand why I would want to do this. This isn't a feminist statement. I just don't see how anything can come above comfort when it comes to choosing clothes. I avoid anything where I'd have to wear a posh frock; I find them too constricting. And I am hopeless at walking in heels. Even though I have a job which offers myriad opportunities to go to parties, openings, award nights and many other seemingly interesting events, I generally find myself turning them down or agreeing and then flaking at the last minute, in part because of the clothing issue.

I own two little black dresses, one for summer, one for winter. They both came from L.K.Bennett and I begrudged so much spending the money on them. How many lovely grey jumpers or pairs of pyjamas could I have bought with the money? Still, they were a practical purchase. They'll last for years and won't date and, because I so rarely go out, people will forget they've seen them before.

Should I try to dress more often to please Tim? Is it a romantic thing to do? If you asked him, he would probably say that I simply don't have the romance gene, while he is biologically programmed to crave that kind of attention. Not the Hallmark hearts and flowers kind, but long, lingering glances and something indefinable that I'll never quite manage to understand. A closeness perhaps or a passion, a feeling of oneness that seems alien to me.

Years of being with me have eroded this in him. His needs are consigned to a locked folder on his desktop in which he never looks. My lack of response was the death knell for anything more romantic. For that I feel guilty. I simply don't know how to respond to the kind of sweet nothings other women seem to crave. I panic that I'm meant to say something back and that I'll flunk it.

I sometimes see him looking at me when we're in the office together. He'll turn from his bank of Mac screens and stare at me and sigh while I am typing on my laptop. I don't understand what the look means but even after all this time it sometimes scares me slightly.

'Are you angry with me?' I'll ask. 'Have I done something?'

Just as I cannot recognize my own emotions, his are utterly foreign to me too. He seems to have so many. They can come on quickly, seemingly without warning. One minute everything is fine, but the next he can be angry or bored or ecstatic. I find it disconcerting, destabilizing.

Often I question if he'd be happier with someone else. Someone who could see wonder in a meteor shower or a dragonfly dancing on the breeze at the edge of a crystal clear river. Someone who would get up at 3 a.m. to swim in phosphorescence in the moonlight. Someone who would enjoy the onslaught of light and sound at a gig. Someone who feels, rather than thinks.

He says not. That he is happy with the way things are, but I am uncertain. We are a team, that's for sure. I produce his photo shoots and he edits my copy. It's part of the glue that holds us together. If we ever split up, he'd need to find someone who could obsessively work out what the light was going to do at any given time on any given day, remember the contributor release forms, charm people into giving their all and make sure lunch had been thought about.

In return I would need someone who could cope with my need to control my environment, who could give me the kind of space I need to operate within, could cope with my shutdowns and my need to logic my way through the world. He'd also need to know exactly how to handle a red pen and give up any pretence at politeness. I prefer criticism to be delivered honestly, quickly and brutally. In that respect, Tim never fails to deliver.

Do I give Tim enough? Probably not. Being with someone who lives almost exclusively in her head must be hard. Always playing second fiddle to my latest obsession cannot be easy either. The truth is that I don't know and I'm not sure I want to ask him. In the early stages of love it's easy to ask someone how they are feeling, to take the temperature of a relationship. Later, there's much more at stake.

A newspaper editor once asked me to include a line about how Tim felt about our relationship for a piece I had written about my autism. I asked him and he summarized it well.

He said: 'It's as if I've been on the same first date for twenty years.'

He craves the easy intimacy other people seem to have. Sometimes I watch long-established couples in restaurants and notice the easy silences – how do they cope without words? – or the way they seem to dismiss the things the other says. I can't get how they can be so impolite to each other and seemingly not care. Occasionally they row and this sends my adrenaline spiking.

I refuse to argue with Tim. I'm sure a psychologist would say this is unhealthy, that arguments are good, that they clear the air. But I just can't do it. We are all, of course, the product of our genes and our environment but the idea of confrontation makes me feel as if my very existence is under threat. I have no idea whether my autism is to blame for this, or whether it's down to the fact that my parents argued frequently, but the result is the same. I have left jobs because people were difficult. I will apologize for things that are simply not my fault. I will leave the room. I will go to bed. Anything not to have to witness or be part of emotions running riot.

Sarah Wild believes the issue is one of anxiety about possible outcomes. She says: 'It's really common for Aspie girls to refuse to argue and not be able to deal with any difficulties in relationships or friendships. It can be that things are not going very well, but they can't address them as they can't control the outcome. They don't know how the situation will play out because they don't know if that friendship or relationship will still be there after an argument.

'Sometimes it needs a third party to mediate that conversation. There is a real emphasis here on building friendships and relationships and maintaining, repairing and closing them. They are going to need to know how to do all these things.'

Tim has described previous relationships as being more passionate, with screaming rows and blissful periods of making up. More of a rollercoaster than the smooth, easy ride I offer. I just don't get how couples can scream awful things at each other and then be passionately kissing only hours later. How do they do that? Surely the bad feelings take much longer to process?

CHAPTER ELEVEN

September 2016

I didn't plan to have a big family, but can now see that having four children worked well for me in terms of dealing with my autism. We are a team. The children foisted a degree of sociability on me and naturally enforced routine into my life. There are bedtimes, mealtimes, waking times. Everything is done to a schedule. Having people depend on me has kept me on track. I genuinely believe it is what has stopped me from going over the edge, from falling. As if I hung on with gritted teeth and could endure anything the world threw at me. For the sake of the children. As they have grown older, and their needs fewer, I have lost my routines and have become more chaotic.

In those hazy days when they were small, or the heady days of a houseful of teens, it seemed impossible to imagine a time when it would end. When they would no longer be there. When the phone would stop ringing at ungodly hours with someone on the other end begging to be picked up. When I would no longer hear the sound of their footsteps on the floorboards above my head.

Today, the house is full of noise and havoc, the kitchen worktops a tangled mass of sweatshirts, headphones, open cereal boxes, books and skateboard trucks. In the sitting room, cushions from the sofas have been left on the carpet, next to discarded socks and pizza boxes from last night's takeaway. Upstairs, toothpaste oozes from tubes without tops and loo seats are left in the up position. In the boys' bedrooms, half-eaten packets of crisps provide nourishment for the mice and Edward Scissortongue's brand of hip-hop provides a bassy backdrop to the beautiful, idyllic chaos we call home.

Soon it will not be like this. A quiet will descend. An awkward, uneasy, unwelcome hush that is suffused with absence.

The boys are leaving for university and that will be it. My child-rearing days will be over. That they are going together feels like a body blow. What will my role be? I became a mother when I was just twenty. I have never had an adult life without a house full of children. I do not know how I will cope with them gone. The sadness reaches my bones. It penetrates parts of me I didn't know could hurt. The pain is visceral. M's feelings wheel doesn't have words for this.

I have been lucky. I have experienced few losses in my life. Application of logic tells me I am not losing the boys – that they are simply moving on to the next phase of their lives. It is a good thing. Of course it is. But it hurts like nothing I've experienced before. I feel the pain everywhere from my heart to my limbs. It's there when I go to sleep and, apart from those blissful feeling-free moments of waking, it is there in the background all day.

Nostalgia comes from the Greek *nostos*, meaning to return home, and *algia*, meaning pain. It literally means homesickness, but we use it for some reason to mean looking back. That's how I feel: homesick for a past I can never find again.

I know I'm being ridiculous. My sense of logic tells me so. Toby will be in London and I am there a couple of times at least, pretty much every week. He'll want me to buy him suppers at Pizza Express, probably more than he ever did when he was at home. Jack will be in Brighton, a city I visit often. We have Facebook, Messenger, Twitter, FaceTime, Skype, iMessage and – the boys' last resort – the phone. It's not like the days when you dropped them off at halls and didn't hear from them for weeks.

I know many non-autistic mothers struggle with this time, but autism seems to add another layer. The loss of control over my environment and my emotions unnerves me. My obsessions aren't helping me in the way they normally do. None is sticking. Like the rest of the country, I have given up trying to second-guess what will happen over Brexit. Work is hectic and I am confined to my desk or kitchen table. But my job is a constant, not an obsession that takes me away from my feelings.

I can accept change when it happens incrementally. In baby steps. I can accommodate new situations if they change bit by bit. The children leaving is brutal. One day they are here, filling the house with music, laughter, dirty laundry and the chemical warfare that is Lynx Africa. The next they will be gone.

Sitting at my desk, writing, and looking at where their boxes have piled up and mingled with each other, I wonder if loss is cumulative. If each new loss layers onto the last, making it somehow more painful. I have only experienced real loss once in my life before. The kind that hits you like a juggernaut. I had a close friend I met through work. We gelled, laughed at the same things, railed against the corporate environment and just connected. We were friends for around nine years. He was tricky, emotional and difficult, but somehow it worked.

Toby was around ten at the time and I was about to take him to the dentist. Finishing work half an hour before we were due to leave, I idly scrolled through Facebook while making a cup of tea. My friend had died. A plane crash.

I remember each second of the next few minutes as if it is happening now. I can still feel the warm mug in my hands, still taste the scalding tea on my tongue. Staring at the screen on my computer, I saw my friend's face on Facebook. In post after post. Then, slowly coming into focus, the letters RIP.

As if sleepwalking, I got Toby into the car. I was in shock and all I could do was concentrate on driving the few miles to the dentist. In the back of the car, Toby was chattering away about how brave he was being, how he was off to the dentist to have 'the worst thing done'.

I switched on Radio 4. My friend's death had made the news. When I had only seen it on Facebook I was able to believe it might be a mistake, that somehow wires had got crossed. Now, in the car with an overly excited ten-year-old, I had to face the fact this was really happening. I scrolled

162

through my brain, trying to remember any time the BBC had got something like this spectacularly wrong. I couldn't think of one.

It simply hadn't occurred to me how final death is. How instant a change it brings to life. I couldn't cope with the speed with which it had happened. Looking back on this time, I can see how my autism played a big role in my being unable to accept what had happened. I can't anticipate how I will react to a situation. I never imagined a loss would cause me to feel these painful and confusing emotions. I realize it sounds ridiculous, but I just thought I would carry on.

Seeing the very obvious signs that the boys are moving out feels so similar to how I felt when my friend died. Shock – even though we have been moving towards this moment since the children were born. Fear – I am unable to contemplate what life will be like without them here. Grief – they are being wrenched from me by the future.

Empty nest syndrome is real; many mothers experience it. The difference is that I don't have people to lean on in the way other mothers do. I rarely see my extended family. I find family gatherings difficult and overwhelming. I don't have a close circle of friends. Tim and I are in different places. He is optimistic. Happy, for them, that they will be embarking on a new adventure. And excited, for us, that we will gain some freedom and the space to find our new level.

I find this difficult to understand. We have always been free to do whatever we want. Sure, it will take less planning now we won't have to be arranging lifts for the children, but other than that, nothing has changed.

I can't understand what the point of me will be once the children leave home. It's a thought that creeps up, takes hold and won't leave me. If the hands-on daily mothering is taken from me, what, in evolutionary terms, is left? I have fulfilled my biological role. I have successfully raised the children to adulthood. I am done.

Where did the years go and how was I not able to control

their passing? When you are knee-deep in small children it feels as if it will never end, that you will never be able to dash to the loo alone, that there will always be warm, sticky fingers clutching on to your calves, so your walk becomes a bizarre straight-legged limp.

Time has done this to me, the cruellest of things. It has taken the children who sat on my hip and touched my face with their pudgy fingers and has turned them into something between a boy and a man. Time has taken them from me and my heart is breaking.

When I feel bad about something, I mainly shut down. I need to be alone, somewhere cool and preferably dark. Ideally I will go to sleep. I can't process an event if I am talking about it or if someone is trying to help. Generally, if there is something that will make the situation OK, I will think of it myself.

On the eve of Jack leaving, I feel so overwhelmed. I go upstairs to my bedroom with my laptop to write. I can't take the feeling of being hemmed in by the office chatter. I need space and peace.

I've been upstairs for half an hour or so when Tim comes in and sits on my bed. He tries so hard to say the right thing.

'It's not long until the Christmas holidays,' he says. 'So it's really just a matter of weeks before the boys will be home again.'

I say nothing.

'It's such an exciting time for both of them. Can't you try to focus on that?'

Again, I don't reply. Of course I have focused on that. I did everything humanly possible to get them on to their courses, which wasn't easy, as they didn't quite have the grades they needed. I don't know what I'm feeling. All I know is I can't cope.

He looks at me in the way one would at a malfunctioning washing machine. I understand this. I am rarely emotional so he has no blueprint for dealing with it.

Feeling bad for both of us I say, 'Let's stop this now before it becomes a futile game of you trying to make me feel better and me pretending you have.'

As he walks out the door, I realize this probably wasn't a very nice thing to say.

Control of my environment is incredibly important to me, but I am careful not to try to control those around me, to let them do what they want to do and be what they want to be. I fear nothing more than someone taking control of my life and would hate to do it to someone else.

Sarah Wild believes Aspie girls are at risk of being taken advantage of, but also that there is the potential for them, in turn, to take advantage of others. She told me: 'Not willingly or knowingly, but quite often girls I come across need a high level of control over their lives and that can come into their interactions with their friends, family and boyfriends. Everyone ends up doing it the way they need it to be done. They can end up with a relationship where they are really directing the agenda and taking a high level of control over the other person. That's OK as long as everyone is happy with it. It can be difficult if the partner is thinking, *If I don't do it this way she's going to have a really adverse reaction*. That can put a lot of pressure on the relationship.'

I do this by living quite separately from everyone else in my life and I can see this wouldn't be an ideal situation for others. I need my own bedroom and my own bathroom, something many people find strange and wrong.

I just don't think it's natural for two humans to sleep together. Surely we need space and calm to be able to recuperate and get the proper restful sleep we need? I'm sure there are people who can sleep curled romantically around each other, but it seems to me everyone else is making a pretty big compromise.

Just as is the case with neurotypical people, many autistic people want to marry and have a family and lots of us do this entirely successfully. Relationships are hard work, regardless of our neurological make-up, but autism brings both benefits and challenges into a partnership. Autistic people won't play games. They'll tell it how it is and can be fiercely loyal to a fault.

The day we take Jack to Brighton is a sunny Tuesday morning. It is early September. Tim and Jack argued about how to pack the car. A predictable clash of wills.

'I don't think we should put my vinyl in the boot,' Jack says.

'It'll be fine,' Tim replies through gritted teeth, anticipating the possibility of having to unpack the entire boot, which has been filled with Tetris-like accuracy.

Despite getting off to a tetchy start, the journey goes smoothly. 'We've made good time,' Tim says. It is a dad remark he feels compelled to make every time we leave Norfolk.

I've seen photographs of Jack's house online, but the reality is better. A tall Regency building a short walk from the sea-front, it has the look of a wedding cake. His room is the smallest in the house and we want to make it nice for him. We've known all his housemates since they were small. They grew up together. In many ways they are creating in Brighton their lives as they were in Norfolk. By moving together en masse, they have taken their childhoods with them.

We go to Tesco and buy new bed linen, towels, cups, plates. Everything Jack will need to survive on his own. Later, Mary arrives with her parents. Even though she and Jack have been dating for more than a year, we have met only to have quick chats when we dropped the children off at each other's houses. Now here we are, watching our babies move in together.

We take Jack to a sprawling second-hand furniture shop to find a table to put his record player on. Inside the cavernous, higgledy-piggledy warehouse Jack and I see the most beautiful bookshelf. It's painted in my favourite colour, a deep grey. Jack and I have always shared a love of books. We often pass books on to each other. He has taken too many to Brighton and stacks of them are piled by his bed.

'Let me buy it for you,' I say. I want to make his house as much like home as possible.

He agrees and we have to fit it into the car. It turns out three people and a large bookcase won't fit into a VW Golf, so I offer to stay while they drop it off back at the house. The warehouse is next to a park with a small children's paddling pool. I sit on a bench in glorious September sunshine and watch young mothers looking over their toddlers as they run and splash, sending balls of liquid light into the air.

I take out M's feelings wheel and try to identify my emotions. My eyes settle on *hopeless*. I think I feel this. At least I feel no hope. Something is coming to an end and endings hurt. *Hurt* is also there. This does hurt in the most visceral of ways. I don't feel *betrayed* or *hostile* or *irritated*. I do feel devastated.

I believed nothing could hurt more than Jack leaving home, but then we dropped off Toby at his university halls. The building and his room were better than I had expected and his flatmates looked like ordinary teenagers, not the hostile strangers I had imagined on the long drive down to London. One was sitting on a step loudly explaining to anyone passing how he had consumed an entire bottle of Jack Daniel's and wasn't sure he was feeling very well at all. A couple of girls sat either side of him offering sympathy, advice and a large take-out coffee.

The move revealed quite how unlike other families we are. The others seemed to arrive with a couple of suitcases and a sunny disposition. The dads made dad jokes and the mothers carried boxes of kitchen essentials. We arrived with enough computer equipment to fit out NASA mission control. With Lucie, who had decided to join in with the move, we made a dozen trips from the car to Toby's new room before we had fully unloaded.

We passed other families on our trips. We watched as two guitars and an amp went in. One student, who had clearly arrived earlier in the day, had a collection of plants that wouldn't have been out of place in Kew Gardens. They are in boxes outside her room. They look beautiful and fragile in this somewhat brutalist building. I wonder if they will survive the term. I feel sad for them and for me.

The children (for that is how they look to me) are buzzing with energy and uncertainty. Parents are making practical suggestions, their charges rolling their eyes and wishing their mothers spoke a little more quietly or their fathers didn't laugh quite so heartily.

We shared rueful smiles with other families as Lucie, Tim, Toby and I politely fought to be the one in control of operations. No one won. The entire move was carried out with gritted teeth and forced politeness.

Once everything is in, we go to Pizza Express in Greenwich for an early supper. Toby orders the same menu items he has since he was three years old. Garlic bread with cheese and a plain margherita pizza with no dried herbs. I feel a pain rising in my throat. The one that signals tears might come.

I go outside for a cigarette and look at a female Aspie group on Facebook. I joined a while ago, but have rarely posted. I once heard Bryony Gordon speak about her book *Mad Girl*. She talked about the importance of *finding our we*. Here on Facebook, I have my *we* – a group of women from all over the UK who think and feel as I do. We are of different ages and backgrounds and have a world of different experiences, but we inherently understand each other. It feels as if it could be a safe place. Perhaps here there is nothing I can say that won't be understood. I don't post anything, but resolve to get more involved once I am home.

After supper, standing outside Toby's halls, he hugs me awkwardly. He hates hugging. I don't love it, but after years of working in the media where you can be ambushed by a hug from someone you met only an hour ago, I can cope. This hug, though, is different. Neither of us tenses up. Feeling him warm against me and sensing how nervous he is, I feel as if I am hugging his three-year-old self. I'm not sure I love like other people. I guess none of us really knows how anyone else actually experiences emotion, but right now I am sure I feel like every other mother dropping off a first-year student. It is strangely reassuring.

He says goodbye to Lucie and Tim and I watch from the car as he tries and fails to open the door with his brand-new electronic key fob. I resist the urge to go and help. I watch his back until he walks through the door and I can no longer see him. Lucie leaves to catch the Tube back to her flat and Tim and I begin the long and largely silent journey back to Norfolk.

I cry on the way home. Tim isn't used to this. In our twenty or so years together he has seen me cry only a handful of times.

'Can't you be excited for the boys?' he asks as we join the M25. I don't tell him that I can't understand how to be excited for someone else. I think it makes me sound weird and uncaring. I love them. Of course I do, and I want them to be happy. Actually, that's not quite right. I want unhappiness to be absent from their lives. I don't want them to feel disappointed by anything. It is as if because I brought them into the world I need to ensure they're comfortable within it. As when you have guests to stay, I want to make the experience as nice as possible for them. I have invited my children into the world and now I need to make it as welcoming and unjarring as possible.

I ask how he feels and he says he is 'excited for the boys, but sad'.

It seems amazing to me that he can distil his feelings into these two simple words. Excited and sad. Mine feel like the sort of equation you see written on a huge blackboard by Stephen Hawking. I cannot begin to unpick or unravel the complex and myriad feelings darting through me. I know one of the feelings stings like a paper cut and another feels like a dull ache. I am sure one feels like panic and another like a heavy loss. I can't tell Tim this. I find it almost impossible to talk about my feelings, even though each day I work at identifying them. They belong to me and talking about them would somehow leave them open to being misunderstood.

We make it home by ten-thirty, which is the time I have my bath. The familiarity of my routine soothes me slightly. I cry a little in the bath, but it feels alien to me and I feel a little self-conscious even though I am alone.

In bed I look at Twitter and my phone flashes up a message from Toby. *I've met some nice people and we're playing drinking games.*

I realize that if they are playing the game called I Have Never he's going to get pretty drunk. His life has been a sheltered one. In the hall's kitchen he was confronted for the first time with a microwave and an induction hob. Having only ever cooked on a battered old Aga, I feel I haven't adequately prepared him for life in the real world. I hope he finds someone nice to show him how to use these new appliances.

I fall into bed exhausted. I realized a while ago that I use logic to try to conquer emotion. Right now, in bed, cosseted by familiarity, I am trying to hold back the tide of emotion until I feel strong enough to logic my way through. I fall asleep by eleven-thirty. I wake with a start at 4 a.m., my face wet with tears. I didn't know it was possible to cry in one's sleep.

The next morning the pain is visceral and immediate. The tears come and I can't stop them. I feel panicky and out of control. I go to get coffee and my order is slightly wrong. The coffee is too strong. Tears track down my face below my dark glasses.

I go home and it feels so silent. There's an absence of the low thump of bass that signals a teenager is home. I cry as I load my bed linen into the washing machine. Nothing can interrupt my Sunday routine. Later I will paint my toenails. I will have to decide whether to move to the autumn colour this weekend or wait until next. Another change is probably too much to bear, so I will stick to the summer colour even though the lawn is peppered with the orange leaves that signal a change in the seasons.

In the office, Tim has his headphones on. He is editing music. I stalk Toby on Twitter and see that he has posted that he likes his halls. I am happy for him and hopeful it will all work out well there. Feeling two sets of conflicting emotions – relief that Toby seems happy at beginning his new life and the icy claw of grief I feel for myself – is almost impossible to bear. It is overwhelming and confusing.

Lucie texts and tells me her friend's sister, who has just gone into her second year at university, has had her student house burgled. No one living there had insurance. Suddenly I feel I have left my two children out there alone in a danger-ous world where anything could happen. I offer Lucie advice to pass on. I tell her it's likely the girls in the house will be insured on their parents' home policies and they should check. I explain exactly what they should say when they complain to the letting agent who had been tardy in giving them the code to the burglar alarm. I feel more in control. I like the practical nature of the conversation. I am once again dealing in fact. I don't know this girl, but I know her sister and want to try to help make things OK again. All I ever want is for everything in the world to feel safe and normal and usual.

Life, though, is messy, painful, complicated and full of ups and downs. How can I cope in a world that is so disorderly? Things are changing too quickly. It's not just the boys going. Post-referendum, the country seems different somehow. People on social media are angrier, less tolerant.

The boys' departure has left me with a sense of being adrift in a changing world. I run into a girl who used to babysit for them. She is now a mother of three. Hers are still small. She has twins at prep school and another at nursery. I can see in her eyes that she cannot fully comprehend what it is like to be left behind when the children move on. Her days are still full of frantic hunts for gym kit, meaningless squabbles over whether Superman would beat a dinosaur in a fight and an endless chorus of *what's for supper?* Is this *envy?*

Overhead, bruise-black clouds are loitering with intent.

I want to tell the person in charge up there that there has been a mistake, that I am not able or ready for this. To lose two children to the world in a fortnight is too much. Surely there is someone who can make this different?

I don't let the boys know I am sad. They have an idea, of course, but I shield them from how bad I am really feeling. My messages are light and breezy. They know I miss them, but they don't know I feel as if I am spiralling fast into a pit of nothingness. They don't know that I cannot find anything good to hang on to anymore. That there is nothing to look forward to.

I think neurotypical women insulate themselves against this all-consuming pain through strong female friendships. They will have at least one or two people they know will be there for them whatever happens. I have only one female friend with whom I could talk about how I am feeling, but I see her rarely. Maybe once every eighteen months or so. She has just moved to Brighton, the town that has taken Jack from me. It feels like enemy territory.

I work hard to remember the advice I have been given in therapy over the years. *Lean into the pain.* I try. I really do. But firstly, what does it mean? And secondly, when I try to stop fighting the pain it washes over me in waves. I would do anything to make it stop.

My usual strategy is to distract myself, to find an obsession and work it hard. Today there are none. I flick through Twitter, looking for something to spark my interest. Nothing does. Maybe this is a different kind of pain, one which won't respond to usual strategies.

My friend Will messages and asks how I'm coping. I reply: *I'm OK.*

Why do I find it impossible to tell the truth? Why can't I say I am in agony, that the pain is real and physical and I want to call an ambulance? Why can't I just tell someone how utterly bleak the world looks to me now? I wish I could explain that I feel I have no purpose anymore. The rest of my life is stretching out before me like an open road and I feel utterly lost. I have no map for this. I entered my adult life with a child on my hip and I don't know how to function without their proximity. The smell of the boys is already fading in the house. I consider going to the supermarket and buying Lynx Africa and spraying it in the hallways, like air freshener. I miss its cloying scent catching in my throat.

I can't bring myself to go into their rooms. I want the doors closed. Tim wants them open. We compromise and they are ajar. I avert my gaze as I walk past. With the doors closed I could imagine them in there, living amongst a jumble of pizza boxes and knotted cables.

I try reading about empty nest syndrome strategies. They seem trite and unhelpful. They suggest getting to know your spouse again. Are they seriously suggesting that two people can live together for twenty years and somehow forget to know each other? They also suggest taking up writing or pottery or even reinvigorating your career. This advice feels rooted in the 1950s, when mothers had no life outside the home. I have a life. It is full. The space the children have left cannot be filled by learning to basket weave.

A small quiet voice in my head says it could be filled with friends. I ignore it. I read instead about grief. We think of grief only in terms of bereavement and it would be an insult to parents who have lost a child to suggest my pain is anything like theirs. However, I do think I am grieving the loss of a part of my life I am never going to get back. I miss a fat little hand in mine, pulling me away from what I am doing to take a look at froglets at the base of the cherry trees. I miss the wonder in a small child's eyes.

I have taken no time to process anything that has happened over the past few years. My illness, my autism diagnosis, the changing shape of my work life – many of those I have worked with for almost two decades have recently moved on and I miss my daily contact with them. I am struck by the Colin Murray Parkes quote we are all familiar with the Queen having

173

used. *Grief is the price we pay for love.* I look it up and the full quote reads: *The pain of grief is just as much a part of life as the joy of love; it is, perhaps, the price we pay for love, the cost of commitment.*

I guess this is the point. The only people I have fully committed to are my children. They have everything of me. My love for them is unconditional and pure. I try to remind myself that pain is the flipside of the good bits. It doesn't help.

I read C. S. Lewis's *A Grief Observed*. He writes: *No one ever told me that grief felt so like fear.* Everything I feel lives within this one line. It explains everything. Once again I am experiencing my main autistic emotion: fear.

My boys leaving has reawakened other losses, but worse than this it has allowed me to imagine losses I am yet to face. It is terrifying. I don't know how to look after myself through this. I cope badly when I cannot see every answer to every question clearly laid out in front of me.

This desire to quash pain at any cost can lead to addiction. It's one of the reasons I barely drink. Years ago, I was worried I was drinking to stop myself feeling. It wasn't a lot – maybe a couple of glasses of wine each evening with supper. But it made me uncomfortable. Most people would, I'm sure, simply cut down or have a few dry days or weeks. That is not my way. Instead, I took control and signed up with Alcoholics Anonymous and worked through a number of the twelve steps.

I realized early on that I wasn't an alcoholic and told some of those I met at AA. They said that I should keep going to meetings as long as I was getting something out of them. I quit drinking and certainly felt a lot better. That was early in 2012 and I can count on one hand the number of drinks I've had since then. In my handbag I still have the AA coin, celebrating that, at least once, I had actually joined something.

In Waitrose car park, I receive a text from a friend, someone I used to work with. She reminds me that on this date last year I was interviewing celebrities live on stage in front of a huge audience. How on earth is it possible I can do that without a second thought, but find it impossible to tell anyone how I am actually feeling?

Right now, more than anything, I wish I weren't autistic. I wish I were like everyone else. My otherness feels like an enormous burden. I walk around the house going from room to room for no reason at all. I don't know what I am hoping to find, maybe something to take away the void that seems to have opened up in my chest.

I want someone to talk to so badly. I tweet in the darkness about how my nest feels empty. A woman I don't know sends me a message. Her name is Nina. Her words are soothing, comforting. I feel myself relax into the pain. *I do feel for you. I've been there.*

Finding My Answers – Summer 2015

The sun is streaming through the window, causing dust to dance on the air. It sparkles. I want to reach out and grab some, in the way I caught dandelion seedpods as a child. Someone told me that if I caught one I could make a wish. I long to wish myself out of this room.

I don't reach out into the glistening air. I don't waste a wish. Instead, I sit still and concentrate hard on what the woman opposite me is saying. I struggle to take in her words. I can hear my heart beating in my ears. I feel dizzy, unanchored.

I believed I was ready for this moment, but her words – muffled by the roaring in my ears – still have the power to shock. She is a consultant psychiatrist. She is telling me why I am the way I am. You are not broken, she says. You are not defective. You are different.

Relief, elation and sadness overwhelm me. More often than not the mercurial nature of emotions stops me from being able to identify them. Today, though, there is an unusual clarity. For perhaps the first time, I understand how I am feeling.

Dr Somayya Kajee, my psychiatrist, is trying hard to catch my gaze. I turn to look at her but can't read her expression. I think it is one of concern.

'Are you OK?' she asks. Her voice is quiet. A soft, pale pink sound.

'How do you feel about this?'

'Fine,' is all I can manage.

Somayya is the kind of woman I have always longed to be. She is graceful, intelligent and compassionate. She is wearing a pencil skirt, crisp, starched shirt and heels; the kind of outfit that would bring with it a level of discomfort that would make it impossible for me to think straight. I'm wearing jeans, a soft cotton T-shirt and trainers – my uniform. In winter I add a soft grey jersey.

Winter is a million miles away. The world outside is bathed in sunshine. It's the kind of day when one seeks out water. Swimming in the sea, lazing on the banks of a river, or sitting by a lake watching dragonflies dance. It's an outdoors day. One filled with the kind of hopeful anticipation that a first date brings. It is not a day to be sitting inside a psychiatrist's office.

I look around the room. It is yellow. I feel small within the space. I am processing the news and I feel a mixture of relief, elation and overwhelming sadness. Usually I am not good at putting names to my emotions, but today I feel a strange clarity around them.

I am relieved because – after decades of uncertainty, confusion and questions – I have the answer as to why I am the way I am. It feels good to have finally told someone the truth about why I think and feel the way I do. I have spent the past five hours honestly answering questions, rather than adopting my default defence of trying to say what I believe the person opposite me wants to hear because it makes me sound normal.

I am sad because I can't help but wonder how much easier life might have been had I been given this information years earlier.

I am scared because I cannot work out if this changes everything or nothing.

I have always known that I'm different. I have blamed myself for not being able to fit comfortably into the world. Not being able to do easily the things others seem to find come naturally to them.

Over the years I have attributed this difference to a chaotic childhood, an addictive personality, my being adopted, not listening at school, a fundamental character flaw, not being blonde and all manner of other nameless faults.

Now I have the answer I don't know what to do. I am aware that soon I will have to leave this safe, warm room and go back out into a world that in some ways is more alien to me than ever. I will have to carry on with my life. I step out and go to find my car. As I walk along the pavement, the early evening sun hits my bare arms.

My limbs ache from having sat still for the past five hours and my head is whirring. I cannot hold on to a thought. Every sound is sharpened: the slam of a car door, the shriek of a girl wearing dungarees as she spills a little of her pink frappuccino onto her T-shirt. A boy punches her gently on her shoulder and I hear the clink of the metal as his watch touches the button on her jacket.

A woman is walking a beige pug. Her heels are hitting the pavement in a repeated pattern: click, clack, click, clack. The dog makes an unmistakable pug-like sound. A snuffle. The pattern becomes click, clack, snuffle, click, clack, snuffle. A small lorry reverses into a hotel car park, its warning alarm beeping. I am hearing each individual sound and it's making me want to get away as quickly as I can.

Random thoughts zip through my mind. Will my name go on a register somewhere? Will they still let me drive? Should I tell anyone, or keep the news secret? Will my husband leave me? What will the children think? Have I been a bad mother because of my autism? Will I get a disabled sticker for my car?

I have been waiting my entire life for this moment. Now I have the answer, I don't know what to do. I call Tim.

'I'm autistic,' is all I can think to say.

CHAPTER TWELVE

October 2016

On the drive back from the coffee shop I see a skein of geese flying over the farm. They are in two V shapes. The one at the front is large. The other, further back, is smaller. In the middle of them is one solitary bird. I feel an affinity with this lone goose.

I stare skyward at it, its tiny silhouette surrounded by activity, by other geese working together for a joint goal. It feels to me as if it is calling *wait for me* to the group in front or trying to hang back so he is scooped up in the crowd of geese behind. That solitary goose is part of something, but on the edge. Not quite fitting, but not able to completely break free and do its own thing.

Before my diagnosis, I had spent all my life waiting. Waiting to find out what was wrong with me. Waiting to fit in. Waiting for my life to begin. Waiting to find the proper me. Now, a year on, I realize I have been waiting for nothing and, like the middle goose, I will probably never fit in.

There isn't another life waiting for me. I've been longing for my real life to begin and have been hit by a sudden realization. This is it. There is nothing else. I am a forty-something woman without the cushion of children at home. Living in the middle of nowhere. Unwilling or unable to allow others into my life. Too scared to make changes, my life will go on in suspended animation.

Why can't I just be normal? It doesn't seem fair. I spent so long not knowing why my body and mind felt so askew. Then I get the answer, only to be told there is no cure. This is it.

I sit on the sofa in the dining room trying to work out

where I can turn for help. Who can I find to rescue me? I have tried love and that didn't fix me. I've tried AA and that too didn't work. I've tried therapy but am still processing my time with M. I tried throwing myself into work, but I am tired and need new challenges. Two incompatible positions.

I'm not sure if I have hit rock bottom, but I know the only way from here must be up. I can't contemplate falling any further. I have never strived for joy, just neutrality, but even that seems out of my reach right now.

I am reminded of Sylvia Plath's plea: *Please, I want so badly for the good things to happen.*

Tim has talked of my kind of existence being life in the grey, but I've realized he is wrong. When things go along smoothly, I feel as if my life is pastel coloured, either pale blue or pink. It's not jolting, but calm and pleasant. Increasingly, though, this place is harder to find.

I know one can't tackle every problem at once and I know I am starting from a point where I have no energy, but I have to try to get a grip and make things a little better.

I am exhausted. It's October and I haven't yet had even a single day off this year. Work is a big stress. The landscape is changing. Some of our clients are spooked by Brexit and have put planned projects on hold. We aren't earning enough money and if something doesn't change soon, we are going to be in stormy waters financially. Tim's optimism means he believes something will just come along and it will all be OK. We are creative people, he says, and something has always come up. I have no such confidence. I think we make things happen and, while luck can play a part, we have to put ourselves out there so luck knows where to find us.

There's another twinge in my chest that I am trying to recognize. I've been working hard at colouring in more spaces on the feelings wheel. I shade *disconnected* in green. It's more than that, though. It feels more melancholic. I realize as I am pouring myself a glass of water that it is loneliness.

Tim and I are disconnected. That word again. We live in the

same house but move separately. When he is watching wildlife programmes in the sitting room, I am in the study writing. When I am in the kitchen making supper, he is in the office playing guitar or writing songs. When I call him to tell him the food is ready, he says he'd rather have it in front of the TV. We can't reach each other.

I feel the absence of the boys keenly. The silence of the house – something I have longed for all my life – merely underlines the absence of their noisy chaos. I find myself switching on the radio just to hear voices from another room.

I have neglected my life and things are piling up. I am late in doing too many things and I am panicking. A magazine I work on needs its pages filling, but I cannot find the energy or mental resolve to begin. This is autistic inertia at its most pernicious.

I am feeling burnout. Years of working too hard and not being able to switch off mentally are taking their toll. I have an infection in my left eye. It is pink and sore and when I inadvertently look at the light it sends a searing pain into my skull. My neck aches from bending over my laptop. My limbs hurt from lack of stretching. I sleepwalk from bed, to work and back to bed again. Cracks are beginning to form, but no light is coming in.

My isolation is becoming more complete. Cobwebs form around the house and it is as if they are taunting me, showing me how much like Miss Haversham's my life has become. When did it shrink so far?

In my younger years I tried losing myself in groups of friends, but it was too overwhelming, too exhausting. Slowly and imperceptibly people began to fall away. I stopped returning calls or replying to messages. Now I rarely see anyone on a purely social basis. I have hunkered down, but not in a good way. Tim and I have no joint friends. We don't do the usual thing of seeing couples. We should have built a circle by now. A circle to encase us, not exclude us.

Without the children, the shape of our lives has changed and we don't fit together any longer. I don't want to be this alone, but I don't know how to change it. From the outside my life looks so different to how it feels on the inside. Others see me as hugely social. I know a lot of people. I have opportunities to do all sorts of things, but somehow I cannot say yes. There's a difference between acquaintances one can hang out with and proper, nurturing friendships. The kind I fear and avoid.

Maybe M was right. Maybe I do need to allow more people into my life. I remember someone saying once, in AA, that they had stuck a quote above their bathroom mirror. It read: *Only you can save yourself.* What if this is true? What if it has to be me?

I hear Tim leave the house to walk the dogs. 'You're such a clever puppy,' he says to Smudge in the voice one uses to talk to a small child. Smudge is nine. In dog years that's sixty-three. Older than me by quite a lot. I like the voice. I like the feeling I get when I think of how much we baby Smudge.

I am reminded of an interview I did with Arabella Carter-Johnson. She is the mother of Iris Grace, a hugely talented autistic child whose paintings have been compared to those of Monet. It was a quick interview for a 'what it's like to' page for a consumer magazine. For this kind of piece, I would usually spend around fifteen minutes on the phone chatting to my subject. I spoke to Arabella for an hour and a half. Her manner was so soothing as she told me how she creates a soft, safe world for Iris to explore.

Would my life have been different if my autism had been discovered earlier and if I had been parented in the same way as Iris? I think of Sarah Wild and the way the girls at Limps-field Grange are prepared for the world. Maybe things would have been better for me, but what does it matter now? I can hardly pitch up at Arabella's front door and ask her to adopt me, or enrol for classes with Sarah.

Feeling hopeless, I wander into the office to check my emails. There are Twitter notifications, a couple of press releases for creams guaranteed to zap wrinkles, a few LinkedIn invitations, lots of junk, and vouchers for Pizza Express. Now Toby is no longer home they don't seem worth redeeming.

There are 8,590 unread emails in my inbox, slightly more on my phone and 5,000 on my iPad. Every day these numbers make me feel guilty and out of control.

The thoughts about my childhood won't leave me. I want to press the reset button on my life. I want to restore my factory settings and go back to the start. Without really thinking about it, I create a new folder for my email on my laptop. I call it 'old mail' and move the eight and a half thousand emails into it. My inbox is now empty. There is no nagging number beside it. All I can see is pristine white. It makes me feel calmer.

I select all the emails on my phone and press delete. Within seconds they all disappear. Then they come back again. I wonder if it's like that with life. I try again and the same thing happens. Maybe there were just too many for the system to cope with. I begin deleting them one by one. It will take hours. I give up. Perhaps I can do a few hundred each day until there are none. Or maybe I should look online and find a fix so they can all be gone immediately.

Tim joins me in the office and opens the music production software on his Mac. I think of sharing with him how I'm feeling, but pull back. I pretend to be working as I take in how tired he is looking.

His moods are cyclical, but have been much more stable as he has got older. When depression descends, though, its grip is tenacious. I have been so wrapped up in the political landscape, the children leaving and in myself that I haven't noticed the telltale signs. His temper has been shorter of late. Conversation has been less. He has been eating and smoking more and he has been more lethargic. He's still been playing tennis twice a week, but has been going on fewer long dog walks, instead throwing balls for Huxley and Smudge in the garden.

While Tim's moods have always been mercurial, he has also experienced episodes of major depression over our time

183

together. A couple saw him hospitalized, while another was so bad we decided we needed to spend time apart. Things had been difficult between us and we couldn't find a place to meet in the middle.

I was spending more and more time away from home just then. Work was going well for me. But for Tim, his period of enforced garden leave had left him feeling adrift, as if he didn't know how to get back into work. He was working with me, but it was always meant to be a temporary measure until he found something more rewarding that would excite him and spark his interest.

Work didn't take up enough of his time and so, in the spaces in between, he wrote songs. They were good. He hoarded them on a hard drive. In a darkened room, usually in the early hours of the morning, he poured all of his emotions into them. The lyrics were the story of our marriage, all his love, pain and resentment flowing out. Sometimes they shocked me. There was so much feeling in them. They told the story of us.

He wrote of our clash of wills, our need for different things and our very different takes on the world. In a track called 'Is it Part of the Deal?' he wrote . . .

> So baby if I wake up mine's a large Jack Daniel's,
>> with lots of ice.
> Crucifix and daisy chains, victims of the vandals.
>> Now that's not nice.
> You tell me you know what it's like as you're filing
>> my life on a spike.
> You tell me you know how I feel.
> Is your arrogance part of the deal?

He wrote of his depression and a feeling, buried deep inside, that he could be a better man. In 'Somewhere in My Room' he wrote . . .

> Somewhere in my room there's a man you've heard of.
> Somewhere in my future there's a man you're proud of.

184

Somewhere in my room there's a world I've dreamed of.
Somewhere in my head there's a space for feelings.

I couldn't understand what it was to be depressed. I could sympathize, but I didn't know how to empathize. I couldn't understand why he would do nothing to help himself. I bounced from therapist to therapist trying to fix my brain and from doctor to doctor trying to fix my body. When they told me I was imagining things, that everything was all right, I didn't doubt myself for a moment. I knew I was right and they were wrong.

I once read that depression is anger turned inward. This might have been true for Tim, I don't know. What I do know is that he turned the anger outward too. He directed it towards anything or anyone that got in the way. Often that was me. The angrier he got, the more I shut down.

It became so we couldn't be together. We agreed something had to change. He had always been passionate about wildlife and the natural world, so he decided to go to university in Reading to study for a degree in zoology.

The idea was discussed for some time until, finally, I thought I was fine about it. I am not good at predicting how any one thing will make me feel. I helped with the practical arrangements and went to Reading with him to help him find somewhere to live. I dug out sheets, plates and pans for him to take. I ordered him some books online. We talked about how he would leave on a Sunday afternoon and come home on a Thursday evening to spend time with me and the boys. He was excited, energized and ready to do something new. I was relieved that the shouting was over and was looking forward to establishing a sense of peace again.

I bought myself a pink Roberts radio, so I could listen to the *Today* programme as I packed the children's lunches and got them ready. The boys were still at primary school. They were surprisingly accepting of Tim going away. They saw the house he was going to live in and liked the black cat they met there.

185

Tim left on a Sunday in September. The weather was still warm and we had spent the day on the beach. It was one of those perfectly memorable days. The sun was warm, the children happy and we walked for miles with our Labrador, Ziggy. We stopped for tea and cakes at a beachside cafe. The children giggled as they ate ice cream. No one squabbled or cried. We felt like a unit. Solid. Us against the world. That evening he left.

I was unprepared for the tsunami of pain that hit me. I felt laid bare without him here. It was a change I didn't know how to accommodate into my life. I felt his absence in everything I did. It was a feeling I couldn't tolerate. My meltdowns increased. Anything could tip me over the edge: a traffic jam, the supermarket not having the only brand of pasta sauce Toby would eat. An unexpected bill. A rain shower. I simply couldn't cope with anything going even slightly wrong.

Tim only lasted two terms. He missed home too much. He wasn't overly emotional about it; he had enjoyed university and the work and could rationalize his being away from home. It didn't matter to him that he hadn't finished his degree. He felt it was a distance we had needed and when he came back he was changed. He had begun taking antidepressants. His mood was more stable. He no longer reacted so quickly or angrily. He had mellowed.

He came home from Reading and we carried on in the same haphazard fashion as before. We found a sort of peace. Life just happened and slowly we grew together rather than apart. In those intervening years we gave in to our eccentricity. We learned to be a family. Now the boys have gone and the shape of our lives has changed we're needing to learn all over again.

Our relationship must appear a strange one from the outside looking in. He craves the exciting, while I long for neutral. He is fiery. I am conciliatory. He welcomes challenges, while I desire the predictable and the familiar. He loves nature, while I find outdoors confusing and overwhelming. He loves making music, while I was told to mime when in the school choir. He is sporty, while I prefer sitting still and reading. I am constantly second-guessing the future. He has somehow managed to find a way to live in the moment, mindful but perhaps with a reckless disregard for the future.

It was around the time that Tim came back that I stopped comparing our relationship to others. It was also the time I stopped actively blaming Tim for all our problems. It is easy to pin everything on the erratic one in a partnership, too easy I think. Because Tim's problems were immediate, loud and difficult, they were impossible to ignore. They meant, however, that I had never had to question what I brought to the relationship. After all, wasn't I the one who was solid, reliable, always there to fix any problems?

Now I worry we're close to breaking point again. I have been so unstable over the past few months and Tim seems to be spiralling down to a dark place. When he is depressed his face looks different. It's a cliché to say the light goes out of his eyes, but it's true. His eyelids become heavier too. As if keeping them open is just too much effort. Everything is too hard for him and my quickness throws his torpor into sharp relief.

'We should talk,' I say when he gets up to put his guitar back in its case. His sigh fills the room.

It's only 6 p.m., but it's so dark outside. We go to a quirky wine bar in our local town. All the restaurants are fully booked. From the minute we walk in, I know it's not going to go well.

The room is too small, too bright. The tables are on top of each other. The voices of the other patrons too loud. We are seated under an air-conditioning unit which is blasting hot air onto us. Although sensory issues can be a feature of autism, they also can plague those with depression. It is as if any additional layer of stimulation from the environment proves too much. I get overwhelmed, whereas Tim gets angry.

He complains to the owner and she turns off the air-conditioning unit. We order our food.

'You wanted to talk,' he says, pouring us both some water.

'I wanted to say sorry,' I tell him. 'I know I've been hard to live with lately.'

'You're just so wrapped up in the boys leaving. It's as if there's no room for anything else.'

'I'm sad.'

'Yes, but you have to get over it and start living. We will find our level.'

'I miss them so much.' I play with my hair, pulling it down over my mouth.

Tim sighs. 'I miss them too, but it's the natural course of things. The alternative – their being here forever – doesn't bear thinking about.'

'I just can't see the point of me now they've left.'

'How do you think that makes me feel, as your husband?'

I sigh. It is a table of sighs. It's always about feelings with Tim. Things can never just be what they are, they have to be examined and dissected in terms of how they make him feel.

'Sorry,' I say.

'We need to find a way to reconnect,' he tells me. 'Can't you see it as having the freedom to do whatever we want?'

This makes no sense to me. I don't think we have any more freedom now than we've ever had. If anything, we have less as we have to be at home for the dogs now the boys aren't around to help out.

'We should think of some things we might like to do together,' Tim says. He seems restless. His eyes remind me of those of a caged tiger. He's looking for drama, for something more.

'I just feel my life is too big and too small all at once,' I say.

Tim looks at me. I mean really looks at me. Not the grazing glances that long-term couples tend to favour, but he really regards me.

'In what way?'

'Well I suppose I always feel I'm running to catch up in terms of making enough money to keep the whole thing going for another year. I feel as if I never stop. On the other hand, I also feel as if the nice bits are getting fewer and farther between. It's as if there's nothing to look forward to anymore. The world disconcerts me. Life has changed too much and too quickly. I don't recognize where I am anymore.

'It just seems as if every day another thing happens and there's something else to worry about. As soon as I manage to deal with something or accommodate it into my life, something else happens. I am struggling to cope and something is going to crack. I feel brittle.

'I feel physically worse than I have for years and emotionally so less regulated than usual. I am tired to my core. I'm sad and I'm sick of my body and my brain. I just want everything to stop.'

I am shocked I have said all this. I put my head in my hands. The food arrives. I find it hard to eat.

'I'm so sorry,' Tim says. 'Things have to change, don't they? Not you. I don't want to change you. The stuff around you.'

Silently I agree. I can't go on like this. I am burnt-out and exhausted. This, I have read, is common in autistic people, particularly those who have struggled for years to 'pass'. It is called *the cost of passing*. It is essentially exhaustion brought on by the extra strain of pretending to be something one is not.

Tony Attwood summed it up well for me. He told me: 'People with Asperger's or autism expend a huge amount of mental energy each day coping with socializing, anxiety, change, sensory sensitivity, daily living skills and so on. So they're actually expending more mental energy. Think of it as an energy bank account. They are withdrawing so much energy throughout the day just by surviving. It is why children at school, for example, have almost no mental energy left for the actual lesson – because they're coping with the sensory, the anxiety, the social.'

Dr Judith Gould, of the Lorna Wing Centre for Autism, agrees. She told me: 'A lot of the women I see are mentally and physically exhausted, with very low self-esteem. They have to learn these social skills. They have to learn how to use the right

189

body language, how to say the right thing. It's another skill, isn't it? Some people are better than others at picking it up. There's a spectrum, a dimension of sociability.

'Neurotypicals don't have to learn to talk about the weather, or those subtle things about social interaction. It's wired within us, but for somebody on the autism spectrum it's not there. You have to learn the social rules. If you're highly intelligent and you have good verbal skills you get by by watching, observing and copying and you appear to be OK. Women and girls are particularly good at masking what is essentially a lack of social instinct.'

I have a high tolerance for difficulties, for unusual situations and for stress. In the past few years I have had surgery ten times, changes in my working life, and two children have left home. I have been told I have a complicated and sometimes dangerous genetic condition and, what's worse, I have passed my EDS on to Toby. I have run a home, worked full-time, been in therapy and have been told I am autistic, something which was at once shocking and liberating. I am exhausted. It is too much for anyone to cope with.

I have dealt with it all as stoically as I can. Not wanting to cause any issues for others, I have tried to bounce back from each setback as quickly and privately as possible. I simply carried on. A week after leaving hospital after major surgery I boarded a plane to Sweden to visit a potential new client. The day after an operation to cure an abscess, I went to London for two days and attended a series of meetings. This, I am starting to see, is not normal behaviour.

I can't carry on like this. I am spent, unhappy and terrified of the future. I want the world to stop. I imagine everything frozen in time and pure silence. This is what I need. Calm, quiet, nothingness. I need space and time to get my head around everything that has happened. More than that, though, I need a path forwards. I am halfway through my life. The rest of it has to be different. I cannot go on like this.

The waitress comes over with the pudding menu.

'Want to share a chocolate brownie?' Tim asks. I nod and he orders for us.

'But,' I add as she turns to leave, 'only if we can have it hot and if the ice cream can be served separately.'

Tim and I share a knowing smile and he puts his hand on mine. I feel a warmth spread through me.

I'm lucky I don't have to pretend with him. I can be myself. If he accepts me as I am, maybe others will too. Perhaps now is the time I need to embrace my differences and stop trying to hide them.

CHAPTER THIRTEEN

October 2016

I'm starting to accept I cannot be perfect. Equally, I hate to make mistakes, to live with the fact that I have done things badly or wrongly. Every one of my wrong steps is writ large in the part of my brain where I store up guilt.

I want to move forward, but I'm held back by what I think might be resentment. My autism might have been spotted earlier – perhaps should have been spotted earlier – and I was denied the help and support I needed. Did I live forty-five years that could have been better?

Tim's view is more pragmatic. 'You don't know it would have been better. You just know it would have been different,' he tells me. 'On the one hand it would have been great to have had more time, with greater awareness of your issues and their root causes. On the other, it might have shaped how you did things and that might not have been a good thing.

'I also think you're emotionally mature enough now to make the changes you need to make. I'm not sure that was the case before.'

I wonder if he is right. I can certainly see the benefits of acknowledging the grief I feel about my late diagnosis and the fact I now have to learn how to come to terms with it. But the realization that I have less time to make the changes I need to make is hard to bear. I'm also aware there will be consequences.

For Tony Attwood, late diagnosis for girls and women usually means a greater number of issues later in life. He told me: 'The trouble is that girls are good at camouflaging it. We often don't pick them up until they're in their teens or older.

'Those diagnosed late or in adulthood have worse outcomes. They didn't get support and understanding at a formative time in their lives. What concerns me is that they created a scaffolding to survive, but that it may not have been the best approach and that sometimes that scaffolding has led to all sorts of issues and concerns, such as depression, low self-esteem, and not having an anchor in society.

'I ask, *When would you have liked to have known?* and they say as early as possible. *I thought I was stupid, mad, bad. I wouldn't have been depressed. I wouldn't have escaped into imagination. I would have handled things differently. I could have explained myself. People would have understood me. I could have been protected.* And, after the euphoria of diagnosis and an explanation, there is the wish that it could have happened earlier. Then there is the fact that the scaffolding has been taken away. What do I put in its place? There's almost a grieving for the lost person.'

I realize I do feel a sense of resentment towards all the doctors who have missed my autism (and my EDS) over the years. But what good does that resentment do? It doesn't help me deal with the feeling of sadness at the opportunities I may have missed and the hardships I might have unnecessarily suffered.

On an intellectual level I am beginning to understand that this abrasive, green feeling will only make things worse in the long run. My autism means I struggle to imagine a future – any future – but what choice do I have? The future is going to happen one way or another. I can't live a *Groundhog Day* life. I must take courage and move on.

It's early and I'm in the office. Tim wanders in, still in his pyjamas. He raises an eyebrow as he looks at a pile of papers on my desk.

'What are you up to?'

'I'm trying to understand myself, to find out what's in my head.'

'Well, good luck with that. I'll come back in five minutes when you're done.' He ruffles my hair as he leaves the room.

As humans we tell ourselves stories. We lie to ourselves. We convince ourselves that we are right or we are wrong or nothing could have made a situation different. But surely the ability to change is within all of us.

My head is starting to hurt and, as a dull autumn light creeps into the room, I realize I have done nothing but waste another morning. Sometimes I will hear a phrase and see that I have never quite understood it before. Today, I think about how I have spent my time. *Spent it*. Like money, I have squandered it. Today is gone and it is never going to come back. It has trickled through my fingers. I can never have that time again.

I must achieve something. I decide to tidy upstairs. Even though I am hugely disorganized and my environment is generally slightly chaotic, I feel so much calmer when it is tidy and there is order.

My eureka moment is suitably prosaic. It comes to me as I am folding some towels that have been on the floor since I took a bath last night. It hits me out of the blue.

All this time I have been thinking that the way to make things better is to become as neurotypical as possible. I have been trying to force myself into a hole in which I will never fit.

As I fold the towels into a neat pile, I think . . .

I am a cat, judging myself by dog behaviour.

It was doomed to failure. I was doomed to failure. And, perhaps worst of all, it was a failure of my making. I have spent too many years trying or pretending to be something I am not and I am never going to succeed.

Whenever I tell anyone about my autism the response is always the same. They are surprised. They can't quite believe it. I seem too much like them and too little like the stereotypical view of autism they know. They think I can't be autistic because I am married. Because I work with words. Because I have successfully raised my children. Or because I don't say anything offensive in conversation. I am not what they expect.

I am not what I expect either and still, a year on from my diagnosis, I am fighting to live a neurotypical life. Where did it get me? Nowhere I wanted to be. I was sad, burnt-out, lonely, demoralized and confused.

The importance of environment begins to make sense on an emotional level. I need to stop trying to be less autistic and start creating an environment in which I can thrive in my autism. I must leave the shadows of an imperfect past and start living in the now.

As soon as it comes to me, it seems so obvious. I have to embrace my autism. I have to accept that there are things about me I will never be able to change. I have to stop imagining the other life that I believed was out there waiting for me.

There is a Buddhist quote I have always loved. Only now, as I line up bottles of bath oils, does it make complete sense to me.

In the end, only three things matter:
How much you loved,
How gently you lived,
And how gracefully you let go of things not meant for you.

In the past I have always thought these lines related to lost loves, success that went to someone else or a material item that was somehow out of reach. Now, though, I get it. I was not meant to have a neurotypical life. I have to stop striving for something that isn't ever going to come my way. I have to stop trying to achieve the impossible and instead work to build – from the ground up – a life that works for me.

If I don't have the inclination to strive for joy, that's fine. That's just how a cat is. I must instead learn to find contentment where I can. I need to look at what I am and what I want to be. It's really as simple as that.

I need to accept that I have made mistakes and, instead of rolling them over and over in my mind, I need to own them, make sure they don't happen again and move on with my life. I cannot be held back by the guilt I feel or allow my mistakes to define me.

If I am afraid, I must not fight against it or pretend it isn't happening. My fear is real. The struggle is real. To minimize it is wrong. It does me a disservice. I must learn to ask for help.

I stare out of the bathroom window. Needing support isn't ugly or wrong. It can actually be quite beautiful. I am reminded of an Instagram post by Rune Lazuli that showed me vulnerability can be beautiful . . .

Crawl into this body, find me where I am most ruined, love me there.

CHAPTER FOURTEEN

October 2016

I feel so much more positive about making the changes I need to make, but am still confused about how to go about it. It's that social imagination thing all over again.

M had asked me: 'Who in your life supports you?' Building an adequate support network was one of the goals I had to set for myself.

I am now turning thoughts into action and am approaching it with an autistic focus. I am spending more time on Facebook and Twitter, building myself a community of like-minded friends online. I have been meeting – albeit virtually – other autistic women. I have been asking for advice on how to cope in certain situations and have been pleased to find, occasionally, that I've been able to offer the odd bit of guidance to them too.

One of the things I find striking is how much pride exists in the autistic community. Steve Silberman once said during a TV interview that autistic adults were leading the 'first civil rights movement of the twenty-first century'. They are. They fight fiercely for understanding and acceptance. Involvement in such a cause, albeit from the sidelines, makes me feel part of something bigger than me. I'm also grateful I have people I can talk to twenty-four hours a day.

I am making an effort to connect more personally with some of the women I've been speaking to online. Among them is autism trainer and author Sarah Hendrickx. When I was at a particularly low point, I rang her and asked for advice on all the things I felt I was getting wrong. She was honest and funny and helped me find a clear path forward.

She told me about the multiple systems she has in place, because she knows that if she doesn't write things down, she will forget. She has a diary, a weekly planner and an online calendar. I've been trying to manage for years with just iCal. She made me see that my approach would never work. I bought a Daily Greatness Planner for work and have been filling in every last thing I need to do.

I have stuck a Post-it note to the bathroom mirror, reminding me to clean my teeth and to cleanse, tone and moisturize. Most days I remember to stick to this routine. Such visual prompts help.

Sarah explained how to *delegate to the future*. She told me: 'I sit down and think, *Does this actually need to be done this week?* If the answer is no, the act of writing it somewhere else – a week or a month ahead – gets rid of it so it is gone and it doesn't bother me anymore.'

Her suggestion has revolutionized the way I think. Whereas once the jobs I needed to do backed up like countless cars in an infinite traffic jam, now they feel more manageable. I am learning to prioritize my way out of panic and I am getting so much more done.

Most importantly, however, Sarah gave me permission to be kind to myself. I plucked up the courage to tell her I had been struggling. That life had overwhelmed me and I was beginning to think that, although I had accepted my autism diagnosis on an intellectual level, I was struggling emotionally. I had all the information I needed, but I wanted now to file it away and get on with living as neurotypical a life as possible.

She said: 'What I always say to people is, go easy on yourself for at least the next six months because it is going to be a roller-coaster ride. You're going to have days when you wake up in the middle of the night and suddenly think about something that happened twenty years ago and you're going to go, *Oh my god, if I'd have known this, then such and such – this relationship, this job, this crisis – wouldn't have happened.*

'That can make you feel furious. It can make you feel devastated. It can make you feel militant. You need to change absolutely nothing until that beds itself down. It's that massive dip of reviewing everything that people go through.

'I say just stop. You are going to experience all sorts of things that you might not expect. It's huge. Absolutely huge. Some people don't need anything beyond that knowledge. I think, though, that many people – particularly women – need to find their tribe. I point them in the direction of blogs, Twitter, Facebook communities.

'It's about realizing you are not alone and there are lots of people out there who get you. When you share your experiences they don't look at you weirdly or frown or say, *you did what?* This might happen for the first time in your life.'

Dr Kajee's advice is that there are small steps that can be taken to improve everyday life. She told me: 'We can all do things every day to make our lives easier. I think for autistic people it's about arming themselves as much as they can with knowledge about who they are and then just trying to live their life like that.

'It's about recognizing that *this is who I am*. My experience is that a lot of autistic people also compensate, so they have mechanisms that they have built up through the years, especially if they get diagnosed later. I saw somebody once who told me they would *put on a normal cycle* when going to a party. A normal cycle means you introduce yourself, you say hello.'

I ask Somayya what families can do to help. 'I suppose the first thing is that families need to be educated. There's knowing what autism is, of course, but it's important for them also to know the person in their family. Who they are and what works for them. That's where they can come together. Families can come to loggerheads sometimes, but usually it's just that lack of understanding.

'I think it's harder when you're younger and you're at school, having to be in that environment. So, the earlier families can recognize and be aware, the better. They shouldn't think *oh, it's nothing*. If you are unsure, if you are uncertain, have it checked out and don't blame yourself. It's not anything you as a parent did. We know it's not related to parenting.'

Of course, I still feel sad that I wasn't diagnosed earlier. That I have to try to make big changes in my life at a time when I should be starting to slow down. At other times, I feel cheated out of the life I think I should have had. These feelings are fleeting, though. Mostly I feel lucky that I have been given this opportunity to know myself better.

In finding other people to spend time with I have stopped expecting Tim to meet my every need. We are embracing doing things together. We walk and cook together now. We binge-watch box sets. We buy each other books we think will be appreciated.

I think about how I would treat someone else in my position and decide it would be with extreme kindness. Kindness and understanding. I have to learn how to take care of myself. But, more than this, I need to allow myself to give up enough control so that I can ask Tim to take care of me when I'm feeling vulnerable.

We're the only people in a tiny cafe. Tim is looking daunted by the full English breakfast that has been set down in front of him. My plate of scrambled eggs with salmon is a little less intimidating, but not by much.

'So, what did you want to talk about?' he asks.

'I want to have a practical session on the things I want to change. In the past I've had such good intentions about changing things, but somehow they haven't worked. I want this time to be different. I know I can be awful, full of big ideas that, too often, I haven't seen through. I know what I'm doing, I promise. I just need a bit of help and I'm determined not to get derailed again.'

'Trump?'

'Why do you say that?' I ask.

'You've been talking about him a lot.'

'Have I?' I hadn't noticed. 'I find it terrifying. He doesn't play by the normal rules. He's so mean to people online and his campaign is so loud and brash and antagonistic. It frightens me.'

'He won't win,' Tim says with certainty.

'Why do you insist on saying things like that? They don't help. You're wrong about Hillary. She won't win the states that matter. I need you to stop telling me he won't win. I know he will. What I really need is for you to help me to prepare for it.'

This feeling – and those which I felt in the weeks after the Brexit vote – isn't all rooted in politics. Mine are decidedly left of centre, but in some ways it's irrelevant in the context of my autism. My pain and fear come from the fact that there seem to be no grown-ups in charge. No one seems to know what's going on, what will happen, when it will happen and what it will mean. The normal rules are being thrown out and I don't know how to deal with it.

Tim gives up on the huge breakfast and pushes his plate aside. I pour some more tea from the pot. 'It's too much change all at once,' I say. 'It hurts my head and makes me hypervigilant. I feel if I turn away from the news or stop looking at Twitter, something else will happen and it will be bad.'

Head teacher Sarah Wild saw evidence of how the Brexit result affected those with autism at her school. She told me: 'It was a very interesting time. I had three girls in here just crying, which I've never seen before. They were really very emotional about it, and were extremely anxious about not knowing what was happening.

'I think they were affected by the fact that people they always thought had a plan – like politicians – actually had no plan. It was as if they thought, *You can look like you're in charge, but maybe you're bluffing*. It calmed down by the end of term, but it was a rough time.

'I think the worst part was when it became apparent that there actually wasn't a plan. The girls thought literally anything could happen. It was as if we'd undone the laws of physics or something and nothing is holding everything together.

'I wonder what effect it will have in the future, on their view of institutions and who is keeping them safe, because at that moment they didn't feel the government was keeping them safe.

'In the end I had to tell them that I am in charge here. While we're all here, we're all safe and I have a plan and can tell you what it is. So let's get on with the things we've got to do.'

It was exactly what Tim had been saying to me: I had to focus on the things I could influence and on my own life, my own everyday.

'I know I'm not meant to talk about politics or Trump,' I say. 'But I want to move past worrying and I'm feeling a bit stuck.'

'It's not that you're *not meant to*, it's that sometimes you allow your obsessions to get out of control. I don't want to take them away from you, I want you to be able to see when they become too much. For the rest of us, but for you too.

'Let's focus on the things we can change and try not to think about the rest.' He pauses and then surrenders to the inevitable. 'I guess we need to talk about money.'

Money is one of those issues we have never really managed to deal with effectively. Most of the time we don't talk about it too much. I worry about it quietly on my own while Tim is always sure something will turn up and it will all be OK.

I've realized our financial situation is worse than I had initially calculated. I go over the sums again and again, often – because I really am not at all equipped to deal with numbers – getting a different outcome.

It is clear, though, that we have to focus on bringing in more money and spending less. I am a financial disaster zone. I don't understand anything about finances, rarely manage to save any money and have never had a pension to pay into. Time is running out. I need to address what is a huge issue, but I am now in the worst possible place to do so. Our lives have bumbled along, earning enough money to pay the bills and a bit more, but with such poor organizational skills I was unable to see the cliff edge towards which we have always been heading.

'Sorry,' I say, 'but, yes, we do need to find a way to spend less and make more. Surely as grown-ups we should be able to manage to deal with this sort of thing.'

One area where I need help is with executive function, which in me is sorely lacking. I find it difficult to structure my day and impossible to plan tasks or estimate how long something will take to finish. I find it difficult to organize myself.

Judith Gould provides an interesting perspective. 'It's being able to plan and organize yourself. It fits in with the lack of social imagination. You're given a task and you have to then work out the best way of solving the problem. That can vary.'

This is an area where I lean on Tim, but I can lean on him more. Ask him to help me to plan my day, my week, the next project. Whatever. I must see my autism not as something to fight, but instead as an integral part of me.

I realize one of the reasons I struggle so hard to deal with change that happens or trying to bring about change is because of my lack of ability to imagine what life will be like if it were different.

I am reminded of the story of an autistic college student. The boy had classes at 8.30 a.m., but the battery in his alarm clock had died. He was concerned he would oversleep and miss his lessons, so had to think of a solution. The one he came up with resonates so deeply with me. He decided to sleep in the classroom at school. He lacked the adaptive skills to replace the clock battery.

I have so many of these kinds of incidents in my life, that I have stopped noticing them. Perhaps the most dramatic was the first time I ever drove in the snow. I noticed my car was behaving differently on this unusual surface. I realized I didn't know how to deal with it. I did what at the time seemed utterly logical. As I lost control of the car, I opened the door and threw myself out.

I was lucky. The car narrowly missed my head and brought itself to a halt by crashing into a tree. Since then I have avoided driving in snow whenever possible. On the occasions I must do so, I inch along at a couple of miles per hour. Until this moment, it has never occurred to me to ask someone to teach me how to drive safely in the snow.

Many autism experts believe daily living skills, such as managing finances, need to be explicitly taught to people on the autism spectrum. Everything most non-autistic people pick up as they go along – how to shop, catch a bus, cook, clean, or manage money – are skills that are difficult for me to acquire simply by assimilation. I need a book, a video or someone to explain and show me how to do them.

There's a perception that anyone with average or above average intelligence will naturally pick up these skills. Strangely, intelligence seems to have little to do with it and one study even found that problems of this kind are especially prominent in those autistic people with greater cognitive abilities.

I have been lucky that I managed to somehow muddle through. The points where my deficits might have been picked up were missed or the people who have helped me have failed to mention how unusual my issues have been.

Every month the phone would be cut off. I had no system for paying bills. In the past, we have had to have a pre-paid electricity key. Even now something unexpected – like a demand to pay the Dartford Bridge toll – can go unpaid until the amount has more than tripled. I cannot adequately explain why this happens.

My bank manager and accountant got together and sorted out a system for me. It was a simple one. I would have two current accounts: one to use with my debit card, the other for direct debits. Rather than paying myself only when I thought I needed to, a set monthly amount would go into my bills account and each week an amount would be transferred over to pay for daily living expenses. The system worked well. At least it did until I started earning less money. It hadn't occurred to me I would have to cut back.

Such flawed thinking is at the heart of my autism. I knew I was bringing in less money, but somewhere the link to that and actually *having* less money was missed.

I posted something about being unable to manage money on a Facebook group for autistic women and got some very helpful advice. Someone suggested going through all my direct debits to see if we still needed everything they related to. Another suggested working out the bare minimum we can live on each week and changing the transfer between accounts to that amount. 'It's called budgeting,' she said.

I tell Tim about this. 'It's not very exciting, is it?' he replies.

I can see his point. This year has probably been the least exciting of our lives. We've barely been out and haven't managed to get away, even for a weekend. I need to make it clear here that Tim and I have never lived a crazily extravagant life. There is no Ferrari on the drive. I have never been on a yacht, let alone owned one. We have been on holiday to Italy or France just a few times in our twenty years together. It is the small things where I fall down. Living with a condition such as autism can actually be hugely expensive. Poor executive function and the inability to plan make doing a weekly shop, for example, a difficult thing to contemplate.

'No,' I say. 'But that's sort of the point. If we can get to the stage where we're not spending money indiscriminately – frittering it away on nothing – we will be able to save some for the exciting things.'

'I looked at our bank statements yesterday,' Tim says, 'and we seem to spend all our money in the supermarket or on takeaways. I actually can't think of anything more boring than that.'

'I think the key to this particular problem lies in forward planning,' I say.

After my diagnosis someone sent me a copy of *The Rosie Project*, a novel about a man with Asperger's looking for a wife. I picked it up yesterday and read it in one sitting. I related to the main character, Don, who has Asperger's, and his Standardized Meal System intrigued me. I wondered if I could adapt it to suit real life. After all, if I could come up with a list of meals for an entire week and work out how to shop for them, I would not only save money, but also hopefully manage to eat too.

'I've thought about some of the things that need to change. I think we need a standard weekly meal planner.' I'd passed *The Rosie Project* on to Tim when I'd finished it, so he was aware of where the idea had come from.

'So essentially you want me to become Don?'

'Ha. I can't see that ever happening. No, we just need to make a list of our favourite things to eat for breakfast, lunch and supper and assign days of the week to them and then write a list of all the ingredients we will need. We write the dates they will be eaten next to them to ensure the perishable items won't have gone off before we plan to eat them.

'Then we need to buy a whiteboard for the kitchen and write the standardized weekly meal plan on it. We will have the same things every day, so we know what to expect. Say, chicken burgers on a Monday evening or pasta with pesto on a Wednesday lunchtime.'

'It's quite prescriptive,' Tim says. 'What if we fancy the pasta on a Tuesday? What happens if we're not hungry on a Wednesday evening? What if we're really hungry on a Friday and the meal planner police say it's prawn salad?'

We both laugh. 'I think it will only work if we try to stick to the right days for a while and then, when we get better at it, we might be able to make some changes.'

'Will it make you happy if we do this?' There is real kindness in the question.

I tell him that I think it will. I tell him that we have to be more organized and that I have to start to eat properly as I'm losing too much weight and feel exhausted all the time.

'Then let's do it,' he says.

Tim offers to go to Waitrose and we write a list. I'm going to try to have a smoothie for breakfast every day, some pitta bread with hummus and tomatoes for lunch then the set supper of the day. This takes some negotiating. Tim hates the idea of eating the same things for breakfast and for lunch and so lists something different for each day. After some compromise on both sides we reach agreement on the suppers.

There's a niggling thought in my mind that I should have known how to do this years ago. Watching Tim outside having a cigarette, I google 'weekly meal plans' and get more than four and a half million results. I thought this was something unique to *The Rosie Project*. Now I see that it's likely most grown-ups have some plan of this sort in place.

'It seems like we're coming quite late to this party,' I say to Tim as he sits down again. I turn my phone screen towards him. 'It looks as if everyone does it.'

He laughs and suggests that while we're here, we put other plans in place.

'It's your turn to add something to the new life plan,' I say. Weirdly I'm quite enjoying this.

'I'd like it if you walked the dogs with me more,' he tells me. 'Getting Huxley was your idea and training him was one of your obsessions when he was a puppy. And you did a great job. We've never had a better-trained dog. But it's really not fair that I now have to walk them both on my own every day. Plus, it would be really good for you to get some fresh air. You have a vitamin D deficiency you do nothing about and getting outside will probably help.'

I like this suggestion less than the meal plan, but agree to going on at least three walks a week. I feel a bit like a child, but realize that's probably because I am behaving like one. The fact is it was me who wanted another dog and I haven't walked him for ages.

The cafe owner comes over and we order more water. Tim smiles at me.

'This could be really good, you know.'

I agree. It's my turn to come up with something else.

'I can't stand living in such a mess,' I say.

'But it's your mess. You don't see the piles of clutter that build up around you, but God forbid someone moves the toothpaste and you can't cope. You insist on clean bed linen every Sunday, then go to bed in a room that looks as if it's been burgled.'

This is so true. The house is too cluttered. I find it hard to stay tidy, but feel so much better in uncluttered rooms. Tim is, by nature, hugely tidy and cannot bear anything to be in the wrong place. If one of the boys leaves a bottle of ketchup in the sitting room he visibly winces.

'OK, so if we come up with a decluttering plan, tackling a couple of rooms per month, will you stick to it?' he asks.

I say I will.

'Your turn,' I say.

'Perhaps we should try seeing more people,' he says. 'We've sort of fallen out of the habit of seeing anyone.'

I am great at work relationships. Better than great, actually. Most agencies that do the kind of work we do keep their clients for three to five years. I have worked with our longest-standing client for eighteen years and the others for more than a decade. Our relationships are strong and work really well.

I need to learn to try to do that on a social level. I am hugely fortunate in that I have people I could pick up the phone to and they would be pleased to hear from me. I could make plans with them, but the idea makes me anxious. What if we arrange something and then I don't feel like it on the day? What if a work thing comes up and I have to cancel? Cancelling anything leaves me feeling overwhelmed. It is almost impossible.

I don't know why Tim has fallen out of the habit of seeing friends. Maybe it's because in many marriages it often falls to the wife to organize social things. Maybe it's because he gets all the interaction he needs playing tennis a few times a week. I think about asking him, but I know he hates any kind of self-examination.

'Shall I say yes to the invitation to Cata and Dave's party?'

'Yes, and while you're at it, I think you should sign up for Cata's yoga classes again. You always feel great once you've been and it's really not healthy for you getting no exercise.'

'OK,' I say. 'And shall I see if Jenny and Peter are free the weekend after the American election? We could go and stay with them in Brighton and see Jack and Mary at the same time.'

All we have done is sort out a bit of a shopping and cleaning routine and agree to make a couple of plans to see friends, but it is as if I have run a marathon. It feels good. Later, when we get home, I start to think about other people I would like to get to know better.

There's a writer called Rachael Lucas, who has also recently come out as having Asperger's. She is working on a novel in which her teenage heroine is autistic. We've been talking a lot online and I'd like to know more. I impulsively send her a message. *Do you fancy a chat?*

She comes back immediately. *That would be great.*

I wonder if she's as nervous as I am. Talking to someone I haven't met before is fine in a work context, but trickier when it's social. It is beyond weird that I think nothing of ringing up someone like Mary Berry or Anna Friel, but would find it impossible to call someone nice I'd quite liked at the school gates or a yoga class.

I'll treat the chat with Rachael like an interview. Another perspective would be great. She picks up the phone after a couple of rings.

'Hello,' she says in a soft and lyrical Scottish accent. I don't know why this surprises me, but it does. We get chatting and it's surprisingly easy. We seem to agree on everything and have had spookily similar experiences. She tells me about her novel.

'It was strange,' she says. 'There was a very precise moment when the idea came to me. I was walking past WHSmith's when a voice in my head said, "I could totally be popular if I wanted. It's not difficult. You just have to look at what they do and copy it."

'When I got home this little voice in my head wouldn't stop talking and I knew straight away she was Grace, the main character in my novel. I'm really sick of novels by people not on the spectrum telling us how it feels to be autistic and using autistic characters as props to make a sentimental point. Whereas in fact, we're just out here getting on with living our lives.

'I wanted to write a book in which the character was autistic but that wasn't the point of the story. It was a coming of age. Will she find a boyfriend? How's she getting on with her friends? The things all young girls go through. She just happens to be autistic.'

I think how much I wish her book had been around when I was a teenager.

'It'll be so cool that Aspie girls will be able to read your book and find a character who resonates,' I say. 'I read loads as a child and teenager, but never quite found someone I could totally relate to. The nearest I think I got was a Jilly Cooper character called Taggie O'Hara. Did you like Jilly Cooper books?'

'Oh my god, yes! To the extent that my son Archie is named after Archie Baddingham. And Verity, my eldest, was very nearly Tabitha.'

'I wanted Toby to be Tabitha had he been a girl,' I say.

Rachael goes on. 'I was completely obsessed with her book *Class* as well. I learned all the proper things to say. I also loved Nancy Mitford's "U and Non-U". People always thought I was quite posh. I grew up on a housing estate in the east of Scotland that was really quite rough. I stuck out like a sore thumb because they thought I was a snob.'

I tell her I used 'U and Non-U' as a handbook for life. It feels liberating to talk to someone so like me and with such similar experiences. We both married very young and divorced. 'I can remember thinking if I got a wedding ring on, I would be a proper person,' Rachael says.

We both went on to have four children. We both find social situations exhausting, but can manage to do things for work that others would find daunting.

'I've spoken a number of times at literary festivals and I've sat on panels at blogger's conferences,' Rachael tells me. 'Before I wrote my book I had a successful gardening blog. Give me a microphone and put me on stage and I'm fine. It's really odd.'

We are both incredibly prescriptive when it comes to the things we will eat and drink. 'If someone makes me a cup of tea,' Rachael says, 'it has to be with fresh water. You cannot reboil the kettle and it has to be poured immediately or I just won't drink it. I realize it makes me sound like a complete princess.'

I relate so much to this. From my coffee order to the way my bed is made, it has to be done my way.

The conversation goes on way longer than I am used to. It must be months if not years since I have telephoned someone for a chat. It feels strange and lovely to have spoken about such ordinary things – everything and nothing – to someone who understands me.

I realize that to most neurotypical people this would sound so strange, but it was such an amazing hour for me. It ends when Rachael needs to go to pick up her children from school. We agree to meet up in London in the New Year. I feel exhausted and elated.

CHAPTER FIFTEEN

November 2016

I'm sitting on the edge of a riverbank with Tim. It's freezing and I can't quite believe I'm doing this. The grass beneath us is cold and damp and the sky is a dirty grey.

'I'm so cold,' I say, shivering for effect.

'Sshh,' Tim says gently. 'It's a bit like fishing. The thrill is in the waiting, the expectation. Without the wait, the moment itself will mean less. It will have no context. You have to learn to be patient. If otters presented themselves on command, the sight of them would be commonplace and ordinary. It is the fact that you have to wait in the mere *hope* that they will show themselves that makes the experience special.

'Oh, and there's no such thing as inclement weather – just inappropriate clothing.' He fishes in a pocket and hands me a warm woolly hat.

Outside, crouched behind reeds, with a bitter wind biting my face? I thought he'd choose warmer things. Thankfully I have coffee, which is keeping my hands warm, and I am bundled up in jumpers and an outdoor jacket, which belongs to Tim. It's huge on me, but I am thankful for the extra layer.

'Just wait until you see them,' he says. 'They're magical.'

I look around but struggle to find anything of interest. Grass, bushes, a line of small trees in the distance and more reeds on the opposite bank of the river. Tim points out a buzzard circling overhead, but for me it is a black blur. Two ducks glide past, but I've seen ducks before. They're just ducks.

We sit for another forty minutes or so, with Tim occasionally bringing his camera up in the hope that something is stirring, me surreptitiously looking for a signal on my phone.

Suddenly, there is a splash in the water and Tim moves the long lens in the direction of a glistening line of fur as it breaks the water and then, in a moment, is gone again.

'Well, that was very special,' I say to Tim but he doesn't move. Then a head pops up, followed by another. Two surface then dive, surface and dive. The shutter on the camera clicks frame after frame as one of the otters leaves the water and sits on the opposite bank. Its face is remarkably cat-like. It has white whiskers and bright, intelligent eyes.

'What's it eating?' I whisper to Tim.

'A fish, I think,' he replies. 'A small fish.'

The second otter catches up with the first and they begin a brief game of chase on the opposite bank of the river.

'Pass the binoculars,' I find myself saying, keen to witness the otters' games in greater detail. A couple more have joined in and they're jumping on top of each other until, with heads and tails blurring in motion, I can't make out which is which.

Tim turns his head away from the camera's viewfinder. 'Some look quite young,' he says. 'They don't take to the water with any confidence until they're around four months old, so I think some of these are juveniles.'

I sit watching in silence, no longer aware of the cold. It is weirdly relaxing. An otter rolls over onto its back and starts playing with a stone. It's making a weird squeaking sound. It's holding the stone over its head, looking at it.

The others join it on the bank. They seem tired after their games and just sit there quietly looking around. I look at my phone and see that an hour has passed. Usually I'd feel too guilty to sit and do nothing for this long.

One of the otters heads back to the water and the others follow. Soon they are all gone.

'Worth it?' Tim asks.

'Definitely,' I say. And I am surprised to find I mean it.

We warm up in a nearby pub. I begin peeling off some of the layers I've been bundled up in.

We decided when making our life plan that we were going to give each other's interests a go. Tim has tons of ideas; I have very few, I'm still learning what my interests are. I've been dragging him into the kitchen more so we can cook together, but I haven't yet discovered a passion I am desperate to share with him. I think this is because all my intense interests are around learning facts. We have listened to some audiobooks together in the car on long journeys and also while lazing around on the sofa at home. I've learned, though, that while for Tim it is about sharing something he finds magical and special, for me it's more about the time we spend together.

'I loved watching the otters,' I tell Tim. 'What will your next suggestion be?'

'Maybe you could come and knock a ball around on a tennis court with me,' he laughs. I'm not sure if he is wholly serious.

'OK,' I say. 'I'll give it a go.' We both know I don't mean this.

'We've had a nice time lately, haven't we?'

'Yes,' I say and think about it for a moment. It's true. Things do feel better. We feel closer. I am being more honest about the things I can't cope with and, instead of getting irritated, Tim is being hugely supportive of any difficulties I encounter.

My lists are working and so is the planner. Of course things aren't perfect. Forty-plus years of behaving in a certain way and the chaos that came with it cannot be erased overnight.

I am taking the first steps though. We've stuck to the weekly meal plan, which means most days I manage to eat healthily a couple of times. We've begun the great decluttering exercise. There are a lot of rooms to go through, but each one that is cleared makes me feel lighter. It is in some ways as if I am curating a retrospective of our family life. It isn't, though, that I pack old Lego sets and Thomas engines into boxes with sadness. Instead, it's with hope for the future.

Deciding what to keep has been interesting. It's as if we have been planning for a future we can know nothing about, an imaginary one. Before I learned about social imagination I would have got rid of all the children's old toys, figuring they were no longer needed. Now I box the better ones or those which were the children's favourites.

'You never know, we might have grandchildren one day,' I say to Tim, who looks slightly horrified at the thought.

I have taken lots of my clothes to a designer reseller in our local town. Over the years I have bought all sorts of clothes, but have only ever really worn my grey jumpers and jeans. It was as if I was stocking a wardrobe for a life I would never have. I bought beautiful heels I could never walk in and would never wear and other items I thought looked nice, but which were simply too uncomfortable against my skin. It felt good clearing out my cupboards and drawers and even better when I was given a nice cheque in return for things that were only littering my life.

Tim is reading and learning more about ASD. It is putting my autism into perspective for him. His understanding of me – and my weird ways – seems to be growing every day. I see it in the small things he does. He is quieter around me. When we go out together he resists the temptation to drive fast. He has stopped trying to explain how I feel or why I feel the way I do and instead has started asking more questions.

It must be annoying for him to have lots of pieces of paper stuck all over the house, reminding me to eat, bath, drink water, go for a walk and so on, but he doesn't say so.

Our relationship feels stronger than ever before. It's as if we crossed into somewhere bad and have now crossed back again. I don't think I considered the impact my diagnosis has had on him. Before I started to learn more about autism and my inability to see things easily from the perspective of another, I would have thought he shouldn't be affected by something that wasn't happening to him. Now I see it differently. While I cannot understand what it is like for him (I don't think I will ever learn that skill), I can see and accept that it has had an effect.

We have met in the middle. We have also seen that each other's ways do sometimes work. I've allowed Tim to take more control of our lives and he's accepted that sometimes my way isn't simply an idiosyncratic quirk. Sometimes it is logical and it works.

We are being kinder to each other. We have become more understanding of each other's faults and we celebrate each other's talents more. Kindness, I realize, is the key to everything and it is in a marriage where it is perhaps easiest to let it slip.

Tim has started writing songs again, this time seemingly from a happier place. I think perhaps he uses music to process how he is feeling at any one time. From the kitchen, I hear him working on a new track. The lyrics drift down the hall and catch me unaware. I recognize myself instantly in his words.

> She's a book without an end
> A pocketful of friends
> An email yet to send
> She's the odd girl in a crowd
> In a world that's way too loud
> Obsessive but unbowed
>
> She's a green light on the road
> Acid for the soul
> Fragments of a code
> A system overload
> She's a spectrum all her own
> Cashmere grey and stone
> Cabbages and rose
>
> She's the hope without a prayer
> The truth before the dare
> A campfire in the wild
> A mother and a child
> She's a whisper and a scream
> A nightmare and a dream

Our conscience in the dark
Politics and art

If M were to ask again: 'Who in your life supports you?'
I would now have a different answer. Tim does, I would say.

I have accepted that my autism, while not totally disabling,
has an extreme effect on my life and I have to take it into
account. That I have managed to muddle through for so long
has been down to luck and sheer grit.

The cracks had always been there, but they weren't allowing in any light. I'm coming to accept now that there are huge
advantages to being autistic – the quickness of my mind, my
ability to take in new information, my intelligence, the passion
I feel for causes I believe in, my inability to take offence. The
list goes on.

I think of Kintsugi, the Japanese art of mending broken
pottery with powdered precious metals. The craft and the
philosophy treat breakages and repairs as part of the history
of any piece, rather than something to hide.

I am flawed. I am, in part, broken. Not by my autism, but
by my insistence on fighting it and by the stresses it places on
me. My being different from most people around me – and the
years of living a life not meant for me – have taken their toll.

I look up pictures of Kintsugi bowls. I see the gold cracks
glistening and realize that without them many of the pieces
filling the screen on my laptop would be dull and ordinary. If
they had been invisibly mended they would always be slightly
inferior, a lesser version of what they once were.

Now, with their imperfections celebrated, they are somehow more. They are damaged and that damage makes them
beautiful.

CHAPTER SIXTEEN

December 2016

The children are home for the Christmas holidays. Toby arrives first. Used to the warmth of halls and having people on hand to talk to all day, he wanders around the house shivering and looking a bit lost for a while. His hand is in plaster; he broke it skateboarding. He brings with him a pile of dirty laundry and his girlfriend, although she stays for just a couple of days before heading off home to Poland.

Tim goes to collect Jack a week or so later. He slips back into life here as if he has never left, splitting his time between home and Mary's house, demanding lifts at random times and emptying the fridge in record time. Tatti is away travelling.

Lucie is the last to arrive. It is always only when Lucie arrives that it really feels like Christmas. Tim and the boys decked the tree while I supervised from the sofa, doing my best to dissuade Jack and Toby from anything too garish. I fail. This year the tree is topped with the head of a toy monkey, the poor specimen decapitated with a kitchen knife. With the lights switched on, the sitting room is filled with festive spirit. But Lucie brings an ingredient missing in the rest of us – child-like excitement and boundless enthusiasm, together with a determination not to allow our traditional Christmas routines to deviate in any way.

'What time are we getting up tomorrow?' she asks. It is a question she has asked every year since she was first able to form the words. It's late on Christmas Eve and she, the boys and I are sitting around the kitchen table. Toby's feet are up and he is rocking on his chair.

My children look alike. They have the same mousey hair,

although Lucie dyes hers blonde. They all have big blue eyes, pale skin and cheeks pink from the warmth of the kitchen. They are mine. Being adopted means growing up resembling no one, so even now I revel in the novelty of these people who are undeniably of me.

We've just finished supper, which is the same as it is every year. Bang Bang chicken, tempura prawns, various salads and pizza for Toby. It is one of our immutable traditions. I love that for three days – from today until Boxing Day – I know exactly what will happen and when. I know what we will eat, the order the presents will be opened in (by age, youngest first), what we will watch on TV and exactly how everyone will behave. It's perfect, but I do see the irony in the fact that the day of the year on which most people want to be surprised is the day I can count on encountering nothing I don't expect.

'Ten-thirty?' Jack ventures, wandering into the pantry to get a beer.

'No!' Lucie says, mockingly admonishing his ridiculous suggestion. 'I can't wait that long.'

'Nine-thirty – and that's my final offer,' Toby insists, toying with a leftover slice of pizza.

Lucie grumbles a bit, but eventually agrees.

Tim comes into the kitchen. 'We're getting up at nine-thirty,' I tell him. 'We've had the traditional debate, but it's been agreed.' I give him what I hope is a look that tells him he should now leave it there.

'Can't we make it ten? Far more civilized,' he says. The children groan, knowing he is playing a game he plays every year. He ruffles Lucie's hair and says, 'OK, Goosey,' to reassure her that he is on board with the plan. Huxley gets jealous and stretches up until his paws are on the kitchen table and his nose is inches from a plate of chicken.

We move to the sitting room. The fire is roaring in the grate and for once the heating is working too. The room is bathed in warmth and the glimmering light from the tree. It's lovely having them all here, sprawled on sofas, eating their way through a giant tub of Heroes.

This house was made for Christmas. It was around this time of year when we first saw it. Between Christmas and New Year, when real life feels like a dream and the days merge in a haze of dog walks in the cold, eating, and watching endless classic films. The family that lived here then had children slightly older than ours, which allowed me to see what it would be like for mine to grow up here. They were all sitting around the kitchen table when we arrived at around 6 p.m. Tim and I were alone.

As soon as I saw the house I knew I wanted to live here. As I stood in the doorway, ostensibly taking in the kitchen, I watched the easy scene playing out and experienced a feeling I found difficult to name. I get it whenever I'm given a glimpse into a stranger's life. It's sort of a cross between embarrassment and melancholy. Within it there is a hunger too. As if I want to be able to take something from the scene and make it my own. I guess it is my long-held desire to know what it is like to feel normal, to experience life in the way other people do. Proper people.

I could see us living here. Tim could not.

'It's too big. We'd never fill it,' he said as we looked around its rooms, ranging from the Georgian period at the front to much older at the back.

We did fill the house. Rather too easily. We grew into it and our lives expanded to light up the dark corners and rooms we once struggled to find a purpose for.

Everything comes full circle. Now, with the boys having left home, it is too big again. Tim and I rattle in its emptiness. The space, though, has given me time to parent myself. I have spent the extra time putting into place strategies that have made life work more easily. Like water allowed to flow, I have found my level.

Lucie, Jack and Toby are ordered to go to bed (another

Christmas Eve tradition) and they trudge off like giant children, complaining jokingly that it's just not fair.

Tim and I organize their stockings, filling them with colouring pencils, stickers, magnets, tangerines, chocolate coins and playful books.

'I can't believe we've been doing this for twenty years,' I say, adding a copy of the Ladybird book, *How it Works: The Cat*, to Toby's bulging stocking.

'It doesn't seem possible.' Tim gets up to pick up a bauble that has dropped from the tree.

'Do you ever wish you could turn back the clock to when they were all small?'

'God, no! It was exhausting.'

It was, of course. But it was also magical.

'We've done a good job with them,' Tim adds. 'Despite everything, they've grown into such great people. We've made mistakes – of course we have – but we are close, they talk to us about anything, and they each have unique characters and unique skills. They're also very funny.'

I add the final novelty plasters, cocktail shakers and book lights to the stockings and curl up on the sofa next to Tim. A recording of *It's a Wonderful Life* is playing on the TV with the volume down.

I, too, have grown up in recent months. I still feel stuck in my late teens – always a girl, never a woman – but I have learned to deal with the world more effectively.

I built myself a sensory kit, something M had suggested. I bought a soft, furry coat and noise-cancelling headphones. I made sure I had sunglasses packed in my bag, even in winter. I used some old gift vouchers to buy a cashmere scarf and made sure I had a block of my favourite scent in my bag at all times. It has made going out so much easier. If any of my senses ever feel assaulted, there is something I can use to negate the effects.

I have allowed myself to feel sad. Slowly I began to accept that, while I don't have the life I had planned and probably never will, I have the life that suits me. I began to count my blessings and started to note down the things I was grateful for. My family. My job. Living somewhere beautiful. My few, but important, friends. My books. My dogs. The autistic community. Audiobooks. Each time something I am grateful for pops into my head I jot it down.

I have learned to think small. I can't control the whole world. The political landscape is not something I can change. All I can do is make tiny, incremental differences where I can. I respond to the parents of autistic children when they get in touch to ask for advice. I write copy for Cata's charity for refugees. I volunteer my time for organizations doing work I believe in. It's manageable. It keeps me out of trouble. It helps me meet new people.

I am working hard to cope with areas of my life I find challenging. I have been breaking difficult things up into bite-size chunks, so I don't either ignore them as being too hard or become overwhelmed trying to deal with them all at once.

I've begun to experiment with clothes. I still wear mainly muted colours and I will never be able to cope with patterns, but I have bought some jumper dresses and even a pale blue coat. I like how it feels to dress differently. It lifts my mood. I still have a host of rules for my clothes: they need to be made of natural fibres; they need to be comfortable; and I need time to accommodate them into my life, allowing them to hang in my wardrobe for a couple of weeks before I can think about wearing them. But it's a start and I think if Tim were to buy me something as a surprise now my reaction would be less visceral.

My planner has become my handbook for life. Every Sunday I sit down and put in everything I know will happen for the week. I plan our weekly meals and we shop.

In my yellow book I list the things most people don't even have to think of. I schedule baths, food, and breaks to go outside. I write down calls I would like to make or messages I would like to send. I limit my time online and mainly look at things that are nurturing. I use the block button on Twitter and don't allow myself to get drawn into conversations with people whose views I will always find abhorrent.

I am being kind to myself.

I can identify so many more emotions on the feelings wheel now. Sometimes they hurt and are unpleasant, but sometimes they are lovely. I still struggle to feel anger. M once told me that unexpressed anger sometimes manifests as anxiety, so I am working on that too.

Tim and I have kept to our *do more things together* plan, meaning I've spent a lot of time outdoors and he has listened to a lot of audiobooks. I feel better for time spent outside. Often it's hard to motivate myself, but I've been on more dog walks. I watched kingfishers from a hide as Tim told me how the young only stay in the nest for around twenty-five days and that the parents only feed them for another four after that. Imagine keeping one's babies close for less than a month.

Later, back at home in the office, Tim uploaded pictures from the day and showed me a video of kingfishers going backwards and forwards to their nest. Over and over again. Each hatchling can eat up to eighteen tiny fish a day. The parents spend all their time collecting fish and feeding their young. It's relentless. In some ways it's not that dissimilar for us. We work to pay our bills and feed our young, often going backwards and forwards doing the same thing again and again.

Since the boys left, I have missed those daily routines, but the kingfishers reminded me how tiring it could be. I have instead focused my energies on teaching myself new skills. As M suggested I should, I have looked for greater support. I began to say yes to invitations. I went to the American Embassy on the night of the US election and, while I was destabilized by the result, I had prepared myself this time.

We went to the party at Cata's. She and Dave are parents to one of Jack's oldest friends and it was lovely to see all the children so grown up. The party was loud and chaotic, with standing room only in the kitchen and sitting room. I stationed myself by the door, so I was able to see my exit route to the outside world. Lucie perched on the arm of a sofa, while Jack disappeared upstairs with his friends and Tim chatted to a man I didn't know. After around three hours I was exhausted and ready to go home, but I had seen how doing a party on my own terms could actually be fun.

It made me feel Christmassy, as does the sound of the children upstairs. Although they are meant to be sleeping, they are actually having a loud conversation on the landing. With the oldest twenty-six and the youngest nineteen, I can't really expect them to be tucked up with the lights out before midnight on Christmas Eve.

'I'll stay up and put their stockings by their beds once they're all asleep,' Tim says, flicking through film options on the TV.

'You could be up for hours. I don't think they'll be sleeping anytime soon,' I reply. 'Why don't I do it first thing in the morning, when I get up to deal with the goose?'

I go into the kitchen to make a cup of tea. When I get back, Tim is half asleep on the sofa. I perch on the arm. In getting to know myself I have got to know Tim better. Accepting my quirks and frailties makes it easier to accept his. He has become more flexible too. He doesn't understand why I won't use green lighters or why my sandwiches need to be cut in a certain way, but he just accepts that it is how it is. I have given up trying to be perfect and, in doing so, have given up trying to make our relationship that way.

Tim raised early the question of what we would be doing on New Year's Eve. It has always been a low point of the year for me. It is the night I feel I have most failed. By not being able to go to big parties. By not having friends to hang out with. Tim's suggestion was that we find something nice to do during the day rather than sitting at home getting ever more miserable. We agreed that we will go for a lovely lunch in London before seeing the matinee performance of *Lazarus*, the musical by David Bowie and Enda Walsh.

It's a good compromise and, for once, I am looking forward to the end of what has been a trying and revelatory year. We feel like a team, as if we've been through something big and have survived.

I look at my watch. It's 11 p.m.

'I'm not sure we've ever been this organized so early before,' I say to Tim.

He opens his eyes and looks at me. 'It helps that we haven't had to read them endless bedtime stories.'

'Don't,' I say. 'I miss it so much.'

I look over to the bookshelf in the corner, where I have kept some of their childhood books. The thin yellow spine of Margery Williams's *The Velveteen Rabbit* catches my eye. Toby loved it best. He would read it clutching his favourite toy, itself a stuffed rabbit called Diddut.

'I don't miss looking for Diddut at bedtime,' I say as I walk over to the bookshelf. 'Do you remember how upset Toby used to get when we couldn't find him?'

I take down the book and begin to read aloud.

'"What is real?" asked the Rabbit one day, when they were lying side by side near the nursery fender, before Nana came to tidy the room. "Does it mean having things that buzz inside you and a stick-out handle?"

"Real isn't how you are made," said the Skin Horse – "It's a thing that happens to you. When a child loves you for a long, long time, not just to play with, but really loves you, then you become real."

"Does it hurt?" asked the Rabbit.

"Sometimes," said the Skin Horse – for he was always truthful. "When you are real, you don't mind being hurt . . . It doesn't happen all at once. You become. It takes a long time. That's why it doesn't often happen to people who break easily, or have sharp edges, or who have to be carefully kept . . ."'

Tim smiles at me, his expression soft in the lights from the tree.

'Well, you certainly need to be carefully kept,' he says. 'Do you feel more real now?'

In many ways I do. It's as if I have come full circle. Initially, I thought my diagnosis was the end of the story, that once I was given that knowledge it would be my happy-ever-after moment. I would know myself and my problems would magically disappear.

What came after was almost the opposite.

'I think I do,' I say, yawning and rubbing my eyes. 'I've sort of learned to know myself.'

'In the end, isn't that what all of us are really looking for?' Tim asks. 'A sense of understanding of who we are and how we got here.'

I suppose it is.

There's a section on the feelings wheel I haven't touched. It has words like *relaxed*, *open*, *warm* and *safe*. While I don't imagine I will ever feel totally relaxed, completely open or even perhaps safe, I do now feel understood, accepted and slightly more secure.

I take my favourite pink pencil and colour in *loved*.

Acknowledgements

A huge and heartfelt thank you to everyone who helped make this book possible. To my psychiatrist, Somayya Kajee, who really did change my life, and to M for helping me make sense of it.

To my agent, Rosemary Scoular at United Agents, for embracing the idea with such enthusiasm and making it happen. To Alison Lewis at the Zoe Pagnamenta Agency for her support, direction and encouragement.

The right editor is so important and the minute I met Carole Tonkinson I knew she was the perfect person to make my book a reality. The Bluebird team have been amazing, so thank you to Laura Carr, Nicole Foster, Rachel Cross and Hockley Spare for all their help in getting the words just so. To James Annal, Wilf Dickie and Ena Matagic for making it look so beautiful and to Jodie Mullish and Jessica Farrugia for letting everyone know about it so brilliantly.

Thank you to all the autism experts who contributed their knowledge, time and wisdom. Also to Louisa Mullan at the National Autistic Society for being brilliantly helpful. Huge thanks, too, must go to all the autistic women who have shared their stories with me and helped me realize that different is most definitely not less.

To my amazing children for being utterly gorgeous and for allowing me to write about them.

To Lucie, Eileen Slattery and Mary Clark, who read my manuscript while it was still a work in progress and offered such valuable input.

Finally, I'd like to thank Tim. Not only for sticking with me when things have been tough, but also for all his help in editing and shaping the story of our life.